SoftballPerformance.com Productions
154 Charlotte Street, Suite C508
Montreal, Quebec
H2X 4A1
Canada

This book has been published with the intent to provide accurate and authoritative information in regard to the subject matter within. While every precaution has been taken in the preparation of this book, the publisher and author assume no responsibility for errors or omissions. Neither is any liability assumed for damages resulting from the use of the information herein.

ISBN 0-61535-498-X
ISBN 978-0-61535-498-9

www.SoftballPerformance.com

SNEAKY SOFTBALL PITCHING

About the Author

"Coach Hal" started out in softball at the age of five. Hal was a batboy for his dad's team and his father was the pitcher. Early on he told his dad that he wanted to pitch, too. He was told to "Sit down, stay out of the way, watch and learn". That is exactly what he did, and he learned really well.

At the age of seven, Hal began taking a ball bag to school with him. Every day after school, he would practice his pitching against a concrete handball court wall. When he was nine years old, the coach of the boys' softball team asked him to pitch for their school team. They won nearly all their games.

Hal pitched for his church team during junior high and high school. There were no boys' softball programs at those schools.

In 1974, after graduating high school, Hal played in his first ASA Men's League in the San Francisco Bay Area. The manager told Hal that the team was not very good but they had a lot of fun. He was correct in both statements. At the end of that season, there was only one nametag at their team's table at the trophy banquet—Hal's. Hal won the Most Valuable Pitcher trophy for their league.

The following year, Hal moved to the Central Valley of California and did not play.

The year after that, 1976, Hal found himself a team. The team was an "A" division travel ball team, a jump of six leagues above the team he'd last competed with two years earlier. The other two pitchers on that team were older, more-seasoned, veteran, major A-rated pitchers. That team stayed together through 1979, winning every league and nearly every tournament they entered. They won the Metro and followed that by winning the 1979 Men's ASA "A" division National Tournament. Hal was voted the Most Valuable Pitcher for the tournament.

Hal started a career in law enforcement right afterwards which prevented him from continuing with the heavy schedule of a travel team. He pitched for several different teams when his schedule allowed. Then Hal was involved in a multiple, roll-over accident in 1986. His injuries took him out of both law enforcement and softball.

When asked, Hal spent the next several years working with some young pitchers. The self-taught train¬ing methods Hal developed for himself were readily passed on to his students. The students learned very quickly and really well. Having watched hundreds of older pitchers during his development, Hal developed a concrete set of pitching tactics and passed these along to even his youngest students. Coach Hal proceeded to write his first book, 'Winning Fast Pitch Softball' in 1999. His tactics drew in students from as far away as Canada, England, Guam, and Australia, as well as other countries, eager to develop the pitching tactics they'd discovered in Hal's book.

Eventually though, those old injuries finally caught up with him and Coach Hal retired from teaching in 2005.

As a youth, when pitching, Hal was considered to be brilliant by his fellow team members. Conversely, he was considered to be 'sneaky' by those unfortunate enough to have faced him. His students were considered to be both brilliant and sneaky as well.

SNEAKY SOFTBALL PITCHING

SNEAKY PITCHING TACTICS TO DESTROY A HITTER'S TIMING

HAL SKINNER

TABLE OF CONTENTS

CHAPTER ONE

AN INTRODUCTION TO PITCHING TACTICS

"Tactics" is a word most commonly associated with the military, used to manipulate the enemy. Here is an example:

Two armies are on the field of battle. One army general focuses his fire at a specific target location in order to drive the other army in a particular direction, the direction the general WANTS them to go. This is a military tactic. The falling shells drive the other army right into the arms of the general's army where they are captured. That marks the end of the battle.

Some would term that tactic brilliant. Others would call it sneaky.

There are tactics in fast pitch softball that a pitcher can use to accomplish the same thing: to cause your adversary (the batter) to do the exact same thing, exactly what YOU want them to do. Many people would call that smart pitching; many would simply call it sneaky. It is smart when you use something that causes you to win, it is considered sneaky when someone uses it against you, causing you to lose. I was considered both smart and sneaky when I pitched, and you will be too.

I am a self-taught pitcher. I developed my own training methods because there were no pitching instructors when I was young. I learned to pitch by watching hundreds of adult pitchers and imitating what they did. I started doing this when I was five years old.

I watched the pitchers who won most of their games and I noted which of their techniques differed from the rest. I also watched the pitchers who were not so successful. Soon I could pick a pitcher's motion to pieces, spotting their strengths, weaknesses, what they were doing right and what they were doing wrong—what were not the best mechanics or what might reveal the pitch in advance.

Most of the teams I played on as an adult were championship teams. We won virtually every tournament we entered. **I pitched with everything I saw other pitchers use successfully and I also came up with and used things other pitchers did not. I developed and** used *pitching tactics* with great success, before teaching them to my students.

It is highly unlikely any pitching instructor out there can teach you much of what is in this book because they don't know of these things; they have not been there and done that. As a pitcher, I learned very early on how to disrupt the batter's timing and how little it actually took to accomplish that. Most coaches, instructors and, sadly, their pitching students are limited to using only a slow change-up to disrupt the batter's timing. Some coaches and instructors think that young girls are not

smart enough to learn these things. I am NOT one of those coaches. I always assumed I was dealing with very intelligent young ladies and I was rarely proven wrong.

You may hear spectators talking about other books and DVDs all the time because they don't care who hears about them; there is nothing threatening their kid's pitching time in any of them. This book is different because this information is NOT in the others. Parents purchase my book and begin working with their kids on a few tactics. They may talk about it to other parents initially. But it is only when they put my tactics to the test in an actual game that they see just how effective they are. At that point, ***MY BOOK NEVER LEAVES THEIR HOUSE AND THEY NEVER DISCUSS IT PUBLICLY AGAIN.*** Those parents don't even want the other pitchers on their own team to have this information and take away pitching time from their kid.

CHAPTER TWO

ONE OF THE TOP REASONS
MY PITCHING TACTICS WORK SO WELL

Human nature is human nature and we are all creatures of habit. Repetition, training, determination and confidence have a lot to do with an athlete's success. How we are trained and the muscle memory we develop play a large role in that success also. What I am about to tell you now is going to be the closest to hitting advice I will offer. It has to do with how coaches and instructors train their hitters. It is about the way they train their hitters on *pitching machines* and it is something that I would estimate 99.99% of them all do the *exact same way*.

The parents, coaches and hitting instructors have those pitching machines whirring. They raise and hold the ball up above the feeder tube for a moment before slowly lowering the ball, then drop the ball down the tube and *schlunk*, the ball comes out and the hitter pounds 17 for 20 to the outfield.

Here is the major weakness they are giving their hitters: they raise that ball up, way above the feeder tube, show it to the batter and then slowly drop it in the tube at a very slow and methodical rate of speed. That speed seldom ever changes. They MUST do this so the instructor can analyze the hitting mechanics of their players.

However, as long as everyone else out there keeps on doing the exact same thing, and training hitters with that arm motion, *MY BOOK AND I WILL TURN OUT PITCHERS THAT DESTROY THOSE HITTERS' TIMING!*

Why? BECAUSE WITH THAT SAME ARM MOTION THEY ARE ALSO TRAINING THE HITTERS TO RELY AND DEPEND ON WATCHING THE PITCHER'S MOTION TO DETERMINE WHEN THE PITCH WILL BE COMING AND HOW FAST IT WILL BE.

That same arm motion also teaches them to rely on the pitcher ALWAYS using the same pitching style for the batter to time the pitcher's motions. As long as these coaches and instructors fail to come up with several different ways to use different arm motions to feed the pitching machines, you will *own* those batters, if you listen to me.

Hitters are mistakenly taught to think (and they thoroughly believe) that they are ONLY watching the hip or only seeing the ball once it gets to the hip at release. That is not the case. The pitcher's entire body is in the batter's view, in their direct line of sight. What the hitters think they see is irrelevant in that respect because they DO see everything, whether they realize it or not. They see the pitcher's motion. I will teach you to use that against them in a very powerful way.

CHAPTER THREE

DEFINING "OFF-SPEED"

OK, I know, I am the one with the often different take on many aspects of pitching. What I consider an off-speed pitch is this: *any pitch where the delivery speed is different than what the pitcher's motions will lead the batter to expect.*

In other words, an off-speed pitch can be a pitch where the motion says fastball but instead something slower is delivered. I also consider an off-speed pitch to include motions appearing somewhat slower while in fact a faster pitch is delivered. That is, the speed of the pitcher's motions is noticeably slower than the actual ball speed.

You will be very surprised at how little that type of intentional difference has to be to make a HUGE effect on the batter's timing, confidence and ability to make contact with the ball.

Any time the pitcher does something to slow the batter's reaction time, the pitcher gains the advantage. Slow that time down enough and **THE PITCHER WINS THAT BATTLE!**

CHAPTER FOUR

BEGINNING PITCHING MECHANICS

This method of starting out a young beginner is not a tactic in itself. However, it is an excellent method to start a beginner off with very strong mechanics, to "tune up" an advanced pitcher or change a step style pitcher to Leap and Drag mechanics. Since the intelligent use of different ball speed is a tactic you will learn from this book, and because the faster you can pitch will make other speeds even more effective, I am starting this book off with some very important advice.

Many years ago I developed the **Coach Hal's "Foundation Method"** for a Leap and Drag pitcher to fix, improve, strengthen, and essentially "tune up" a pitcher's leg work. Soon after that, I tried this same method with some very young, brand new pitchers. What typically took months to accomplish using the beginning pitching methods of other instructors was being accomplished by my techniques in just one or two 30-minute sessions.

I used this method in a clinic once for a 10u team. I only had two hours to work with 14 kids and only two of them had any pitching experience. All of them were pitching hard and throwing mostly strikes by the end of that session. This method is so simple they picked it up instantly. They practiced with what they learned that day and, 30 days later, their team held a pitching clinic for 8u's. *THE INSTRUCTORS WERE THOSE VERY 10U KIDS WHO HAD LEARNED COACH HAL'S "FOUNDATION METHOD"* and they taught it in one session exactly as I had taught them a month earlier.

CHAPTER FIVE

COACH HAL'S "FOUNDATION METHOD"

For most young players, their first attempts at pitching are done in their own backyard with Mom or Dad as their catcher and first pitching instructor. In many cases this first session is not a fun time for either the parent or the child.

Most parents can offer a beginning player some knowledge in most of the aspects of this sport. However, most of those same adults do not have any pitching experience to draw from and cannot really offer much at all in the way of training for a young beginner pitcher.

The parent does not know where to begin and the kid does not know what to do to get started correctly either. This can easily lead to one or both getting very frustrated, often placing a strain on their relationship. *"She's not doing what I tell her to do"* or *"I don't want to do this anymore because he gets mad at me when I don't do it exactly like he wants me to"*. I have no doubt you have heard the same sort of reports from parents who have tried to do this themselves and it did not turn out well at all.

Many times those first attempts end with the young player throwing in the towel immediately, walking away from it and never wanting to try again. I consider this to be one of the biggest tragedies in any sport.

Here is the main problem as I have always seen it. The only thing that is consistent with all very young, brand new and beginning pitchers is this: *nothing is consistent in their mechanics, from one pitch to the next.*

With all the different things a windmill pitcher must do in the mechanics of throwing a pitch, if there is no consistency, how can the coach possibly adjust those things to ensure the timing and sequencing are correct?

Trial and error over a long period of time is the typical tack. However, that long period of time can be one of the most frustrating times in a young struggling pitcher's life. Many give up after a few tries rather than go out and experience even greater frustration by continuing.

Using this method takes the monkey off the parents' backs and puts it on MY shoulders, where it belongs.

Now it is not a case of the parent telling their kid what to do; it is a case of the parent helping their kid do what the pitching instructor tells them they should do. Now the parent is fulfilling the role of

Sneaky Softball Pitching

assistant rather than instructor and their kid will not get frustrated when the parents try to help them learn, as a result. The attached diagram illustrates how I start off a young beginning pitcher. (My beginning students always progress very quickly.)

The pitcher knows where they are supposed to throw the ball; they have a catcher as their target.

What they lack is a target for their stride foot. They have no idea how far to stride out, or where and at what angle their foot should be.

Chalk this diagram on a concrete surface. Draw the pitcher's rubber, a power line and use their stride foot to trace a target footprint for the pitcher to aim their stride foot to when they stride out.

Using this method will enable the beginning pitcher to progress at a far faster rate than normal because they will almost immediately develop consistency and speed in their stride.

Just as you must build a house on a good solid foundation, an instructor must do the same when building a pitcher. The pitcher must also have a good solid foundation to build a pitch from. The pitcher's stride is that foundation.

The stride length must be reasonably consistent for a pitcher to adjust the timing of all else in the pitching mechanics. Once they can consistently come down at the same stride length every time, the rest of what is involved in the pitching mechanics starts to fall into place much more quickly with just a little practice and a little adjustment. They will progress much faster with this method because they know they are at least doing THIS part consistently and correctly.

When working with a beginner pitcher with this (or any other) method, there are two important things to watch for:

1. **<u>Watch where the position of the ball is inside the windmill circle at the exact instant the landing foot touches down.</u>** When the landing foot touches down, look to see that the ball is at least far enough into the windmill circle that it is behind the pitcher's head, just starting into the downswing behind them. If the ball is at twelve o'clock (straight up) or if the ball is coming up in front at any point when the landing foot touches down, this can create shoulder soreness and should be corrected immediately. Most beginning pitchers are a bit awkward at first, and their stride foot landing can be jarring to the body. If the ball has not reached the downswing when the landing foot touches down, those jarring landings that can make for a sore shoulder after practice.

   Have the pitcher practice that timing with a plastic Wiffle softball, the kind with all the holes in it. Have her take a long step and bring the ball up and over her head to about one o'clock at the exact moment the landing foot touches down. Have her freeze her arm as soon as the landing foot touches down. The ball should be just forward of her head in that one o'clock position. It will only take a dozen or so of these exercises for her to get that timing down. ***Having the ball entering the downswing at the instant the landing foot touches down is critical for the safest mechanics for the female shoulder complex.***

2. <u>**Opening and closing the door.**</u> Imagine the shoulders and hips as being a door. When standing on the rubber and facing the catcher, the door is closed (zero degrees). When standing on the rubber facing third base (first base for a left-handed pitcher), the door is wide open (90 degrees). As the pitcher starts her forward motion, she wants to swiftly open the door virtually all the way as she brings the ball through the upswing.

   As the ball powers through the downswing, she closes the door. *However, she must only close the door halfway.* Having the hips at a 45-degree angle to the catcher at ball release is the safest mechanic for the female shoulder complex.

The stride length I use to start a budding young pitcher is calculated as their height minus three inches. The stride length is measured from the front of the pitcher's rubber, to the tip of the toe on their landing foot when it touches down. At a set length of their height minus three inches, this will typically require the new pitcher to *push off* the rubber somewhat, instead of taking a very long and extended step. This may feel and appear awkwardly far for a beginner who is inexperienced at pushing off from the rubber.

The calculation of the pitcher's height minus three inches is a rule of thumb; it is not set in stone. It is the guide from where I start a beginner and may be adjusted to suit when everything starts to click for them and their motions become more aggressive and stronger. In a very short time of consistently coming down at that stride length, that length will undoubtedly extend a few inches. In no time at all, they will begin to perfect the timing of all the other pitching ingredients. When that happens, they will sense it; they will start throwing faster and more smoothly. They will become more and more aggressive with their arm speed, push off and stride length.

After the first practice using this method, draw the pitcher's rubber and the power line but don't draw their footprint target. After they warm up, have them practice a dozen or so pitches and pay *very* close attention to where the toe of that stride shoe reaches. Mark a small line at that point and then measure it from the front edge of the rubber. If that measurement is the same or less than the length it was in the first session, draw a new footprint target the same length as it was during the first practice.

If that length is *greater* than the length used in the first session (and, chances are, it will be), set their new footprint target at the new, longer length and ensure it is at a 45 degree angle (where the door is halfway open) when drawing it.

This will require a third person to watch the stride foot closely if you are operating as the catcher during this exercise.

Sneaky Softball Pitching

Q: *Why start off with the pivot foot at 45 degrees?*

A: When the pivot foot starts at 45 degrees, this will usually compel the pitcher to open her hips during the motion. Many beginners initially pitch with a straightforward approach, without opening their hips. It is a documented medical fact that for the safest mechanics for the female shoulder complex, the hips must be at 45 degrees at ball release. Starting with the pivot foot at 45 degrees helps accomplish this.

Q: *Why must the landing foot come down at 45 degrees?*

A: When the stride foot comes down at a 45-degree angle, this will compel the pitcher to keep her hips at least somewhat open through the release. The landing foot should be at 25 to 45 degrees when it touches down. I prefer my beginners land at 45 degrees to ensure that they DO keep those hips open at release. If the parent or coach follows the instructions and draws out the diagram as it shows, this will be accomplished in almost every case.

For a more experienced pitcher who is not achieving the speed they should, giving them a more aggressively lengthened footprint target may be all that's needed to speed them up and smooth out their motions. This alone can give them the consistency they need, combined with a longer and faster stride length, to achieve the most speed they can get.

There are many instructors that are now using this method with their pitchers and it is getting results faster than anything else they have done. It has also been very well received by the parents of those pitchers. The instructors are giving this out as a loose handout to every new student's parents, even at their clinics. Their kids are improving VERY quickly and the instructors and parents are seeing major achievements at the very first lesson. Simply giving the pitcher that footprint target so they know where their foot is supposed to land and at what angle is the key to quick progression and piecing it all together.

Once the pitcher has achieved that consistency, it is time to go see the professional pitching instructor for an evaluation if they do not already have one. If you work with beginning pitchers and their parents, try this method. You will see quick results. Always have a lot of patience with a young, new and just beginning pitcher. Big improvements CAN be seen in one session but a great pitcher does not happen overnight or in one single session. Make sure your young pitcher/kid has a lot of fun when learning to pitch and make sure YOU have just as much fun while you are doing this as your child does. When they have fun learning and they know the parent or instructor is having fun too, they will want to come back for more.

COACH HAL'S "FOUNDATION METHOD" DIAGRAM

Pitcher: **Date:**

Pitcher's Height:

This description assumes a right-handed pitcher. Adjust accordingly for left-handed pitchers.)

Draw on a concrete pitching surface using white chalk to mark and trace.

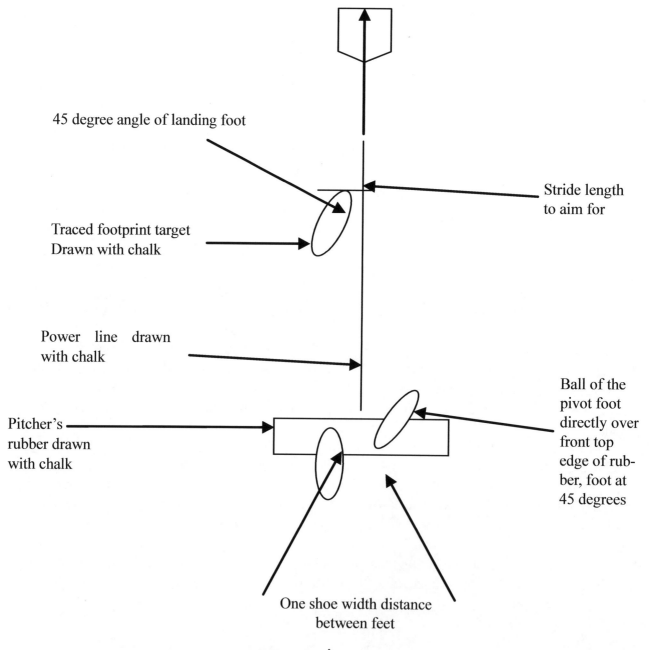

45 degree angle of landing foot

Stride length to aim for

Traced footprint target Drawn with chalk

Power line drawn with chalk

Ball of the pivot foot directly over front top edge of rubber, foot at 45 degrees

Pitcher's rubber drawn with chalk

One shoe width distance between feet

CHAPTER SIX

UNDERSTANDING PITCHING MECHANICS

One of the best pieces of advice I can give to a pitcher is to observe other, more experienced pitchers at work in their games. There is much to be learned by doing this. It is how I learned to pitch.

There are a few things you must know before you can learn from doing this. You must understand what is involved in throwing a legal and completed pitch. There are eight separate steps involved and you must know and understand each of them. When you do understand them, then and only then can you pick a pitcher's motion to pieces.

You will be able to watch for and single out each individual step in any pitcher's motions. You will be able to identify what they do right and wrong—what their strong points and weak areas are; what they protect and hide from the batters; and what they do that will give away the pitch. You will begin to notice the subtle differences in how they throw their various pitches.

As a batter, knowing these steps will enable you to analyze the opposing pitcher and use her weaknesses against her.

You will become your own best pitching coach. You will be able to place yourself in the batter's shoes and analyze your own pitching motions for weak spots, then fix them before the next batter uses one of them against you.

Here are my rulebook's eight steps:

1. **TAKING THE CALL** Always take the call with both hands at your sides. The ball may be in either your throwing hand, or in the glove. You may stand just behind the pitcher's rubber or with both feet on the rubber.

2. **BRINGING THE HANDS TOGETHER** Place both feet on the rubber. Your hips and shoulders should face forward toward home plate. Bring your hands together in front of you at waist height to simulate taking the call. (Most rulebooks instruct you to bring the hands together for one second, but you are, in fact, permitted to hold the ball for up to ten seconds. This indicates to the umpire that you are ready to throw a legal and completed pitch.)

3. **SEPARATING THE HANDS** Separate your hands and remove the ball from the glove. This commits you to throwing a legal and completed pitch.

4. **ARM ROTATION (WINDUP)** Once you begin your forward arm motion you are not permitted to reverse or stop the motion, Neither are you permitted to make a second revolution

with your arm. You are, however, not required to make a full windmill circle. You may drop your hand down and to the rear before starting your forward motion.

5 **THE RELEASE** This is the exact moment you open your hand and release the ball for delivery. This is performed together with Steps 6 and 7.

6 **PIVOT FOOT PUSH-OFF** Push off the mound with your pivot foot. You are not permitted to raise your other foot from the rubber and push off a second time (second pivot point). When pushing off the rubber to take your stride, you must ensure some portion of your other foot, namely your toes, stays in contact with the ground.

7 **THE STRIDE** Take a step with your stride foot at the moment you release the ball.

8 **LANDING THE STRIDE FOOT** The stride foot must come down inside the invisible lines that run between the sides of home plate and those of the pitcher's rubber.

Once you learn each of these steps, act them out one at a time and understand them, then you can watch any pitcher, spot their weaknesses and use that knowledge in your team's favor.

Here are just a few of the things you should look for:

- If the pitcher takes the call with the ball in the throwing hand, does the pitcher give away the call by applying the grip in plain view instead of hidden in the glove? If so, does the pitcher bring the hands together so quick the grip could not possibly be changed? If they do bring the hands together for one second or more, does the pitcher appear to change the grip once it is hidden inside the glove?

- Does the pitcher vary the time the ball is in the glove from one pitch to the next, or is the presentation always the exact same length of time, which makes the pitcher very predictable and easier to hit off of?

- When the pitcher goes into the forward rotation, is the rotation slower with a slow delivered pitch? Does the pitcher ever slow down part of the windup to control runners on the bags?

- Is the angle of the landing foot past what would be 12:00 (Straight towards home plate) to no further than 1:15 (assuming a right handed pitcher)? If it is beyond 1:30, break out the ice packs; this one is going to have control problems!

You will step into the batter's box knowing that pitcher's secret. You will also not reveal any pitching weaknesses of yours to the opposing team because you will have already fixed them.

CHAPTER SEVEN

THE BATTER'S JOB

The batter's job is to hit the ball. As a pitcher, your job is to prevent those batters from doing their job. To do your job, it's important to recognize what steps the batter must take to do his job. These steps the batter must take are:

1 **SEE THE BALL.** The batter wants to see the ball at the earliest possible moment in the pitch so they can set their eyes on it and draw their target. Once they set their eyes on the ball, they track it, from the instant it leaves your glove, through the windup and delivery, until it reaches the bat.

2 **KNOW WHEN TO BEGIN THE SWING.** The batters time the pitcher's motion and the ball's speed in the delivery, and react accordingly.

3 **ADJUST THE SWING TO MAKE CONTACT WITH THE BALL.** Once the batters lock their eyes on the ball and draw their target, they determine when to begin their swing. Then they adjust their swing to accommodate the movement of the ball and the placement of the pitch.

Now, let's look at this logically. By doing some simple math, we can calculate how much time the batter has to do her job.

Let's say this is an age 12 and under game. The distance from the pitcher's rubber to the back of the plate is 40 feet. In this instance, the pitcher, after taking her step, releases the ball five feet from the rubber. The point where the batter will likely make contact with the ball is approximately two feet in front of the rear of the plate. Let's say the ball has a delivery speed of 45 mph.

- 40 feet minus five feet, minus two feet, leaves 33 feet the ball must travel, from the point of release to the point of contact.

- 5,280 feet (the number of feet in one mile) x 45 mph equals 237,600 feet of travel per hour.

- 237,600 divided by 60 (minutes in an hour) equals 3,960 feet traveled per minute.

- 3,960 divided by 60 (seconds in a minute) equals 66 feet of travel per second.

- 33 (the number of feet the ball must travel) divided by 66 (feet of travel per second) equals 0.5 seconds for the ball to travel 33 feet at 45 mph.

Now, that is not a lot of time for a batter to do the three things necessary to make contact with the pitch. The earliest possible time for a batter to see the ball is when the pitcher separates her hands and takes the ball out of her glove. The longer she keeps it hidden, even into the first part of the windup, the less time the batter has to find the target and fix their sight on it.

If the pitcher breaks from her presentation slowly, the batter will see the ball very early in the pitch, lock eyes on it and follow it all the way through the windup. By doing this, the pitcher has extended the time the batter has available to do these things, likely by a full second. The batter now has triple the amount of time to take their necessary three steps to win the battle. Ideally, the pitcher wants to prevent the batter from seeing the ball until the actual moment of release. She wants to keep the ball hidden in the glove until the last possible moment in the windup. The batter must still accomplish all three steps to succeed. Reducing the time available to do this makes the batter's job *much* more difficult.

Here's a fact you probably haven't realized: the moment the batter realizes when to begin her swing is ***entirely controlled by the pitcher!*** Batters have ploys to attempt to break a pitcher's rhythm, concentration and timing. They can turn to face the pitcher as she brings her hands together to make the pitcher suspect the batter is going to bunt. They move around inside the batter's box or suddenly call for a time-out. There are many hitting tactics to distract the pitcher and prevent her from doing her job.

A smart pitcher will have many more tactics to use against the batters. The hand is indeed quicker than the eye. It takes a measurable amount of time for the eye to focus on something, send that signal to the brain which makes a corresponding decision, and then send that signal out to the body's muscles to react.

That is a lot to do in less than half a second. The less time a pitcher gives a batter to make those determinations, the lower the batter's chances are of making good contact with the ball, and the better your chances are of striking the batter out.

The pitcher must be able to analyze herself and her pitch; to see herself from the batter's box, the batter's view. The pitcher is the only offensive player when her team is on the field.

So, if you wish to improve your pitching, you must take a good long look at your pitches. Consider having someone videotaping the pitches from all angles to help you analyze your strengths and weaknesses. Identify what can be adjusted to limit giving the batter any unnecessary opportunities or advantages. Fix what may be revealing your pitch prematurely. ***Don't give the batter a single advantage!***

If you have multiple pitchers on your team, get together and pick each other's pitches to pieces. Dissect each movement and evaluate what you do well and not so well.

Look at each pitcher from several angles, especially from the batter's box. Every pitcher has strong and weak points in their pitches and mechanics. The other pitchers on your team will be your best pitching coaches.

Above all else, use your imagination and know the rulebook. Read it carefully and find the loopholes that you can use to change or add something to your pitch, things that will make your pitching unpredictable, more effective, and harder for the batters to read.

You will have a lot more fun when the batters stop having fun because of you.

CHAPTER EIGHT

INCREASING PITCHING SPEED *Now*

The art of constantly changing pitch speed is vital to every champion pitcher. To help you attain this skill, I am going to share with you one of my biggest speed pitching secrets.

Back when I was still in competition, I did many things to throw just a little faster than the other guys. A few days after returning from a deep-sea fishing trip with my dad when I was around 13, I discovered one of those techniques. Among all the leftover equipment lay a few large, round fishing weights. Instinctively, I grabbed one and stuffed it inside my ball bag.

At my next game, I did my normal warm-up routine. The game start time was delayed slightly so, while I waited, I pulled out that fishing sinker and began playing with it. I pretended I was bowling but without moving my feet because I was standing in the dugout. I raised the weight up to the ten o'clock position and then swung it down and behind to three o'clock. I did about 20 or so of these reps just to kill time.

When the game started, I picked up the softball. I froze for a second. IT FELT LIKE IT WEIGHED NOTHING! I threw my five warm-up pitches. They seemed somehow quite a bit faster than my normal fastballs. My catcher came out to me and asked what I'd done because I was throwing really fast. Whatever it was, he said, keep doing it. The first half-inning was short and, at the end, the ball still felt weightless. By the end of the second inning, the softball regained its normal weight but my catcher claimed I was still throwing faster than ever before.

Several innings later, my catcher indicated that, although I had slowed down a bit, I was *still* throwing a little faster than in our previous games. With that in mind, I pulled the weight back from my bag and began repeating the bowling motion, ten o'clock to three o'clock, over and over. And, just as before, the ball felt weightless and I was throwing faster than the preceding inning.

I kept doing this workout routine, after my normal warm-ups, throughout my remaining competition career.

I had all the young pitchers I worked with doing the same thing and the effect is exactly as it was with me.

The weight I used the first time was a two-pound 'down rigger' ball, a round, lead fishing sinker. I later went to three- and four-pound balls, keeping them both in my ball bag. Here are some tips when doing this exercise:

1. Keep the palm facing forward at all times;

2. Take a full 15 seconds to go from the ten o'clock to the three o'clock position *through the bottom half of the windmill circle.*

3. Start with your stride foot ahead of your pivot foot.

4. Lean slightly forward as you bring the ball behind you.

5. Keep your elbow slightly bent at all times.

For those 10 years old or under, I suggest using a one or two-pound ball.

For those 10 to 12 years old, I suggest a two- or three-pound ball.

For older kids on up to adult, most will find a three-pound ball will be sufficient but some find a four-pound ball is a better weight.

For younger pitchers, watch the muscles as they execute this. If the muscles begin to quiver at any point during this exercise, either stop or try a lighter weight. Twelve repetitions of this exercise should take effort but not so much that they cannot finish twelve reps.

WARNING: NEVER ATTEMPT THE FULL WINDMILL CIRCLE WITH THIS MUCH WEIGHT; doing that can injure your shoulder. THIS EXERCISE SHOULD NEVER BE DONE WITHOUT ADULT SUPERVISION and every precaution should be taken to ensure the safety of all those nearby.

THIS IS A SERIOUS AMOUNT OF WEIGHT. YOU AND ANYONE NEARBY CAN BE SERIOUSLY INJURED.

Never lift the weight higher than ten o'clock in front of you and three o'clock behind you.

Never rush this exercise.

I would also suggest, if using a fishing weight, that you cut off the eyelet, file it down smooth and give the weight a double wrap of white medical tape to keep the hands from getting discolored by the lead. Wrapping it in white medical tape also disguises what it is so the OTHER teams don't catch on.

You will be very surprised how effective this exercise is and how much confidence a young pitcher can gain doing this.

CHAPTER NINE

HUSTLE IS EVERYTHING

If you are a pitcher, you are the inspirational centerpiece of your team.

You wield more control of the ball than any other member of your team. When you control the ball, you control the game. Your team looks to you more than anyone else for **their** confidence during the game. They feed off the confidence level you display. When you are fired up, so are they. When you hustle and show it, so will they. Understanding this is not a tactic used against the other team; this is a tactic to keep **your own team** fired up and playing at their best.

If the pitcher has a defeated look or attitude, the whole team tends to give up. The team's level of hustle starts gasping to try and stay alive. The other team senses this and it makes them hustle even more. While you have the ball in your hand, all eyes are on you, **including your own team's**. When the other team sees you dragging, upset or looking defeated, they get fired up, their confidence level rises and they get much more aggressive, on the bags and with the bats.

When you are fired up, excited and show your determination, the rest of your team will be just as determined to win as you are. Once in awhile, when you strike someone out, turn to your 2nd baseman, make a fist, pump your arm and just say "YEAH". Do that a few times during the game and watch how fired up your team gets.

They will want to win for YOU because they know you are trying your absolute best to win for THEM.

A pitcher that is fired up, with a team that is fired up behind that pitcher, is the most intimidating thing the other team will ever face. It takes away their confidence level and when that happens, their level of hustle drops like a rock. The team that hustles the best is always the team that wins the big trophy.

Stay fired up, always hustle and show it.

The pitcher in the circle is where the team's hustle breathes its breath of life from during the game. Don't let it be the place where the team's hustle dies too.

When a team's hustle dies, the pitcher is the only one that can give it immediate CPR with the very next pitch.

Not even your coach can do that!

Stay fired up, show it, be vocal about it and your team will definitely respond. You have a responsibility to your team to do everything you can to win the game. No other player has more responsibility for their own team's performance than the pitcher.

The pitcher is held more accountable for the final outcome of the game than any other player.

Have you ever wondered why the pitcher is the only individual team player that has a win/loss record for their position?

Maybe now you understand why just a little bit better.

CHAPTER TEN

SHAKING OFF THE CALL

Shaking off the call is one of the two simplest ways for a pitcher to become a little more unpredictable.

Shaking off the call and varying the time in presentation, from one pitch to the next, are the very first tactics I teach to a very young, beginner pitcher. I teach these two tactics first, as they do not involve doing anything to the pitcher's mechanics. Every second a batter spends in the batter's box, in their stance, is like an eternity. When they must hold their stance for any extra length of time, they begin to think about things other than the ball. Doing this is a strong tactic at any age.

Shaking off the call is very simple. When the catcher flashes the sign, the pitcher simply shakes her head no. Doing this once or twice, every other pitch, makes the batter wait VERY impatiently.

Here is the simplest way to accomplish this for a beginner pitcher.

Let's say the call is one finger, whatever pitch that may signify. The catcher flashes one finger, the pitcher shakes it off. The catcher again flashes one finger and again, the pitcher shakes it off. The catcher flashes one finger again and this time the pitcher nods her head yes, THEN throws that pitch.

Now the batter has had all kinds of time to think and wonder what the heck the pitcher is up to. The batter will be very tense in their stance, as compared to when they first stepped into the box.

This also gives a very young and beginning pitcher the appearance of being in control, calling her own game and being a very experienced pitcher. This also adds to her intimidation factor over the batters.

This gives a beginning pitcher her first realization of how much control she wields has over the batters.

If the coaches from the other team are trying to pick up the signals, this also helps to throw them off from doing it. They might see what the call is between the catcher's/coach's legs and even alert the batter to it. However, if that call is shaken off one or two times, now they are unsure of what pitch is actually going to be thrown.

Batters rely and depend on a pitcher being predictable. The batters need that predictability to make that huge decision: when to pull the trigger and start their swing.

A pitching student and their instructor must have consistency in the learning environment. That consistency is ABSOLUTELY NECESSARY for the instructor to teach, chart progress, make corrections and to build the student's confidence level.

However, **if that same pitcher takes that same learning environment pitching consistency and pitches with it in the competition environment, the batters will hit the pitches as consistently as the pitchers are throwing!**

Consistency in pitching translates to predictability in pitching to a batter and that gives the batter a BIG advantage. Why would you want to give the batters a big advantage like that? Keep it for yourself and have all the success and pitching fun you can! Don't pitch with consistency.

CHAPTER ELEVEN

MIXING UP THE PITCHING CALLS

If your coach sends the calls to the catcher from the dugout, who in turn sends them to the pitcher, the other team will likely figure out the calls by the second or third inning. No matter how tightly you hold your legs together, it's impossible to hide from someone sitting straight across from you in the other dugout. Maybe the coach has come up with some very elaborate calls that look more like batting signals, hard to teach, hard to learn and easy for your catcher or you to confuse.

Here is a simple way to throw the other team off your calls and keep *them* confused. This will require you to do something you may not do normally and the coach may not be willing to do, depending on the confidence level that exists.

The coach must have enough confidence in your pitching ability and experience to let you make your own decision every once in a while. If the coach can loosen the reins a bit, here is what I suggest.

Let's say the pitcher throws three different pitches and the signs are one, two or three fingers. The pitcher and catcher are adding another call and it is four fingers. When they receive the four-finger sign, the call is anything the pitcher wants to throw: it's THE PITCHER'S CALL. Whatever the pitcher feels comfortable with at the time, it's the pitcher's choice. Your catcher must be able to catch anything the pitcher chooses to throw without knowing what is coming. That is not a problem for a good catcher.

The only rule to follow is this: when the pitcher gets the pitcher's call sign, they should make sure the pitch they choose is not the same one they picked the last time they got that sign. If they choose a drop the first time they get the call, they should choose something different the next time. If they can do that, it opens the door for a real tactic in pitching. Let me explain.

The catcher will now give two signs for every call, a true sign and a false sign. One sign is held between the catcher's legs as normal; the other is flashed across the chest in plain view of everyone. Always make sure the two signs are different from each other. Let's say the true sign for the pitch you are calling is two fingers. The catcher flashes two fingers for the true sign between the legs and four fingers for the false sign across the chest. The other team will not know which is the right sign.

To add to their confusion, trade off every other inning. For the first inning, the true sign is the one the catcher flashes between her legs, the one on her chest is ignored. For the second inning, the sign on the catcher's chest is the true sign and the one between her legs is ignored. This will confuse the other team's coaches but here's where the real fun starts.

Every once in a while, at least twice an inning, have the catcher give the sign for the pitcher's call. When the other team sees three fingers between the catcher's legs and one finger on the chest produce a drop, and then the next inning one finger between the legs and two at the chest produce a drop, they will be confused. At this point they can only assume that one, two, or three fingers, either between the legs or at the chest, is the sign for a drop. When the four-finger sign is given and your pitcher elects to throw a drop, the other manager will tear his hair out and the parents will go completely nuts trying to figure it out!

For even more fun, add the fifth finger as the pitcher's call, too. Toss in one or two batting signs, touch your hat then your cheek, and then flash both signs. When you flash two or more fingers, every once in a while wiggle your fingers when giving the sign.

Now, THIS is something the pitcher should already be doing to be unpredictable. THIS IS ANOTHER PITCHING TACTIC IN ITSELF.

Every third or fourth pitch, have the pitcher shake off the call two or three times. Say the catcher flashes two fingers; the pitcher shakes her head no. The catcher flashes three fingers and, again, the pitcher shakes it off. The catcher flashes two fingers again and this time the pitcher shakes her head yes. This will not only add to the other team's confusion, it will give an inexperienced pitcher the appearance of being in charge and VERY experienced. It will also throw off the batter's train of thought, and they might just step out of the box.

You may be surprised by how many teams you face that rely and depend on reading your signs, picking them up from the dugouts and the stands. Or at how many of the other base coaches will read the signs between your catcher's or coach's legs and shout a signal to their batters.

Have fun with this because it's smart pitching and that is always a blast!

CHAPTER TWELVE

BAD PITCHING HABITS

Here are a few things that many pitchers do that I consider to be bad habits. I will explain why. You decide for yourself if they are important enough to change if they're already habitual.

WARMING UP IN OPEN VIEW. When a pitcher warms up before a game, often times they will do it to the side of a baseline on the infield. This is basically showing off for the fans; a little ego thing. The pitcher and the pitcher's fans enjoy this a great deal but you must realize the other team is watching you, too.

You are right there, in front of everyone, easy to see. If you think doing this is making an impression on the other team, you are right. They are watching you like a hawk, *getting your timing down in their heads*. They are building their confidence with every warm-up pitch you throw. That is not smart pitching. You are giving them a sneak preview. You don't need to show them what you've got until game time. Keep it a secret as long as you can. There is almost always an area to the side of the field that will have a fence or bleachers blocking the other team's view. Warm up there instead.

Always warm up from the distance that you will be throwing in the game, or as close as you can estimate. If you warm up at a much shorter or much longer distance you will find yourself struggling, at least for the first inning, to find the strike zone. As an example, watch the other team's pitchers.

There is always some hot dog pitcher that wants to warm up in the outfield throwing at a greatly extended distance. They look tough; they look scary to the other team. Fortunately for you, that pitcher has to throw the ball with a high arc so the ball will come down in the strike zone. It is almost always guaranteed that pitcher will be struggling to bring the ball down to the strike zone for at least the first inning and possibly the second. That is not smart pitching.

SHOWING TACTICS DURING WARM-UPS. Never throw a slow change-up during your warm-ups. Never throw at one hundred percent full speed during warm-ups. If you utilize tactics as part of your normal routine, don't use any of those during pre-game warm-ups either. Save those surprises for the batters, and don't even throw them during your five warm-up pitches from the rubber. Let them think you are a somewhat slow, easy and predictable pitcher, one that looks easy to hit. Let the other team find out, with their very first batter, that you just declared war on them. Strip their confidence away from them immediately and *don't give it back*. This is a tactic in itself and it is a lot bigger one than you think.

Pitchers and coaches will have different opinions on this. A pitcher is an offensive player while they control the ball. Only if the pitch is hit do they then become a defensive player fielding their position, just like the rest of their team. If you throw batting practice to your own team, never let up, go for the strike out and don't throw meatballs. Don't ease up on them and throw slow easily hit pitches. If you do that you are not helping them or yourself. The pitchers they will face in games won't be doing that and neither should you.

You must condition yourself to think that when you are in the pitcher's circle your job is to strike out the batters, no matter what the circumstances are, no matter what anyone else says.

If you do not treat batting practice like it is the big game, you may find yourself in the big game pitching batting practice to the other team. A winning pitcher does not step into the circle with anything less than full offensive battle mode and intentions. If the coach wants anything less than that out of you, have him pitch to them himself at practice or use the machine.

MAKING EYE CONTACT WITH A BATTER. Never EVER make eye contact with a batter at any time, for any reason. Always stare at your catcher's facemask. This is the prime directive of pitching psychology. The pitcher does not let the batter know they have been noticed as an individual by the pitcher. Imagine if you pass someone you know on the street and when you look at their face they pretend not to have seen you. You feel slighted; it's very cold, uncaring and rude. That is exactly how you want the batters to feel when they face you—that they do not matter to you in the least and you will not recognize them as an individual, only your next victim, the next stat in the score book, nothing more than that.

Making eye contact gives the batter a feeling of confidence; they have been noticed and have had an impact on the pitcher. You made eye contact and showed the batter a little respect by doing so. The batter will interpret your respect as fear and will attack you more aggressively now. Don't give them that edge or any advantage whatsoever. Keep them for yourself.

CHAPTER THIRTEEN

BECOMING AN UNPREDICTABLE PITCHER

Disrupting a hitter's timing is an important part of a winning pitcher's game. It consists predominantly of how the pitcher controls the batter by controlling what the batter is thinking at that exact moment. If you do the math you will understand why. The distance between the back tip of home plate and the front of the pitcher's rubber is laid out in your rulebook. When a pitcher goes through their motions they will normally release the ball approximately four feet in front of the rubber.

The point where the batter may or may not make contact is roughly two feet in front of the back tip of home plate. So, the distance the ball actually travels between those two points is typically about six feet less than the distance called for in the rulebook. This is the *ball travel distance*, the only distance that matters.

For example, let's say the distance is 40 feet, plate to rubber, minus six feet, which equals 34 feet of ball travel time. Let's also say the pitcher throws at 45mph. With this information, we can determine the exact amount of time the batter has from the point the pitcher releases the ball, to the point where the batter attempts to make contact.

Here is the same formula we discussed in chapter 7: $45 \times 5{,}280 = 237{,}600$ feet of ball travel per hour, divided by $60 = 3{,}960$ ft per minute, divided by $60 = 66$ feet of ball travel per second at a speed of 45mph.

34 feet (the actual ball travel distance) divided by $66 = .515$ seconds of ball travel time. The batter, in this case, has 0.515 seconds to: 1. lock her eyes on the ball; 2. determine exactly how fast the ball is approaching; 3. Determine when to start her swing; and 4. adjust her swing to accommodate the pitch placement and path of the ball. ***That is not a lot of time to do all those things!***

If we assume the batter has a 50/50 chance—a 50% chance of making good contact, then a pitcher must do something to increase her chance of winning that battle. The pitcher must take away the advantage the batter has of *knowing when to start her swing*. In this example, if the pitcher can cause the batter to delay that decision by $1/10^{th}$ of a second, the pitcher's chances of winning that battle go up by 22.8%. (.1 is 19.4% of .515)

If the pitcher can do anything, or a combination of things, to cause a $2/10^{th}$ of a second delay, the pitcher's chances go up by 38.8%. The batter's chances have now been reduced to 11.2%. (Remember, the pitcher is assumed to only have a 50% chance of good contact.) The pitcher likely will win as it is highly unlikely now that the batter will make good contact with the ball.

Try this using a stopwatch: start and stop it as close to 2/10th of a second. It can be done but you must be *very* quick. Now try for 1/10th of a second. If you can stop the watch between 1/10th and 2/10th of a second, you will have a better understanding of precisely how little time is needed to delay a batter's decision and win the battle.

Here are a few more examples to help you understand, using the above formula:

> Distance - 40 feet at a speed of 50mph = 0.464 seconds; 1/10th of a second delay = 21.6% increase in the pitcher's chances.
>
> 40 feet at a speed of 55mph = 0.421 seconds; 1/10th of a second delay = 23.7% increase
>
> 46 feet at a speed of 60mph = 0.454 seconds; 1/10th of a second delay = 22.0% increase

Double all those percentages for a 2/10th second delay and the pitcher will invariably win. There just isn't sufficient time for the batter to do what's needed for the batter to win.

Optimally, the pitcher must distract the batter with her motions. With all the pitchers I watch every year, I rarely see any who vary their pitching motion. That makes them very predictable—*too* predictable. I want you to be unpredictable.

Unpredictability is crucial to stay competitive and progress to higher levels of play. Here are my suggestions to you on how to become unpredictable:

1 *VARYING THE TIME YOU HOLD THE BALL IN YOUR GLOVE*. This is the very first tactic I teach a young beginner as it does not require technique. When you are a predictable pitcher, the batters get your timing down and step into the box with a level of confidence that **YOU GIVE THEM**. They step into the box knowing exactly when to pull the trigger and start their swing. Remember I said that the batter must do three things in order to make good contact with the ball: see and track the ball; decide when to begin their swing; and adjust their swing to the pitch. By varying the time you hold the ball in your glove, the period in which you wield total control over the pace of the entire game, you deny the batter any confidence she has in gauging your timing. Therefore, it becomes more difficult for the batter to make successful contact with the ball and get a hit.

If you check your rulebook's pitching regulations regarding "The Presentation," (bringing the hands together), it says something to the effect of "You must present the ball for one second and no more than ten seconds." The exact moment you break from presentation and start your pitch is entirely up to you. You, the pitcher, are in control. How you use that control will determine your effectiveness.

Let's say you hold the ball in presentation for three seconds on the first pitch and seven secon[d] on the next. You've batted for your team and you know what went through your head at that moment. That extra four seconds felt like an eternity in that box. You may have wondered, "What's going on?" or "What is she doing?" "Why isn't she throwing?" "Should I step out and call time?" "Where's my coach?"

When you vary the presentation time from one pitch to the next, you exercise control over the batter's thoughts. You disrupt their concentration by making them think about something other than what they should concentrate on at that moment. They should be focusing on seeing the ball but you are creating uncertainty. You're making them think instead about you. *You* are in control. While they are momentarily distracted, you start your wind-up and deliver.

Here is a simple pattern for younger pitchers just starting out. Hold the ball for three seconds during the first pitch, then seven seconds, then three again, then five, and then repeat.

$$3 - 7 - 3 - 5$$
$$3 - 7 - 3 - 5$$

Once you become comfortable with this, you can mix it up. Like this, for example:

$$3 - 7 - 5 - 2 - 5 - 1 - 4.$$

Vary the length of time between each pitch. Every once in a while throw two or three in a row using the same amount of time, just to break up the pattern and throw the batter even more off-balance.

The batters will often step out of the box when about eight seconds have elapsed, to see if they can affect you. If a batter does this, show no emotion. Stare at your catcher. *Do not make eye contact with the batter*. This tells the batters that you and only you are in control. Nothing they do will have the slightest effect on what YOU are about to do to THEM.

2 *VARY THE BALL SPEED* The second step in becoming unpredictable is to vary the delivery speed from one pitch to the next. Never throw two pitches in a row with the same ball speed. Always either add a little more, or take a little off every subsequent pitch.

Most pitchers I see throw at one of two speeds—either as fast as they can, or as slow as they can deliver a change-up and still reach the plate.

The idea of throwing a pitch using your fastball grip, at anything less than full speed may scare you a little. You have likely always assumed a fastball must be thrown at full speed; anything slower will be easy to hit. *Not true!* Varying the ball's delivery speed from one pitch to the next is just as effective as varying the time you hold the ball in presentation. It throws off the batter's timing and causes the batter to delay her response and reaction time.

When the batters watch you, you will rob them of their confidence if they see you pitch at more than the typical two speeds. They'll get nervous. They won't know how long they have to wait for you to pitch *or* what speed the ball will be moving toward them. They'll hesitate. You control them by creating that hesitation, by making them unsure when to start their swing. Make every pitch an off-speed pitch. Change the speed on each and every pitch.

If your fastest pitch is 65 mph and your slow change-up comes in at 40mph, you have 24 ball speeds that fall between your fastest and slowest pitch speeds from which to choose for your off-speed pitch. If you throw a pitch at 65 mph, and the next pitch at 52 mph, the batter will probably swing too early on the second pitch. If the third pitch is at 57 mph, the batter, having seen a 65 followed by a 52, will likely swing too late or perhaps not at all, because they could not decide precisely when they should start their swing.

Practice different speeds before attempting to use this tactic in competition. It will take a little practice to achieve several different speeds if you have used only two speeds up until now. A good way to develop different speeds is "the wall workout." Throw your fastest pitch against a wall and note how far the ball rebounds before hitting the ground. Then try throwing at various speeds and see if you can vary the rebound distance. Aim for speeds ranging from 100%, or your fastest speed, on down to 80%, 70% and 60%.

Changing ball speeds from one pitch to the next will make you unpredictable and make it difficult for any batter to make contact with the ball. Keep every advantage for yourself; give the batters absolutely nothing that they can rely and depend upon. If your motions, particularly your arm speed, always says "fastball" to the batter but you can, in fact, release the ball at three or four different speeds, changing constantly, the batter has NO CHOICE but to watch the ball travel to determine exactly how fast THIS pitch is coming. **THAT TAKES TIME THEY DO NOT HAVE.**

3 *DELAY THE ROTATION* The pitching regulations in your rulebook say that the rotation of your arm must be a forward motion and cannot be reversed or stopped once begun. *It does not say you cannot **slow down** part or all of your rotation.* It does not specify at what speed you must rotate; merely that you cannot reverse or stop it. You can use this to your advantage as, this tactic not only has an effect on the batters, but it can also draw runners off the bags too early, and helps control the runners and prevent them from challenging you as often.

As a pitcher, you are familiar with what you need to do with a slow change up. You want to make it appear that you are going to release a fast pitch except you slow the rotation down at the very end of your forward wind-up. You deliver a slow pitch to catch the batter off-guard. This has an effect on the batter, although the amount of time between a fast and slow release is too slight for a base runner to react badly and make a mistake.

There is an offensive pitching tactic that works similarly to a slow change-up, except the rotation is slowed at the first stage of the pitch, not at the very end. This is the fast-slow-fast variation of the delayed rotation pitch.

You take the call, present the ball and break from presentation quickly, as if you were going to throw a fastball. As you bring the ball up in front of you, slow the rotation until the ball in your hand is at the ten o'clock position. Then you slow the arm rotation down from ten o'clock to two o'clock, making it take between 3/4 and one full second to complete the slow portion. You then speed up your rotation and deliver a good off-speed pitch at roughly 80% of your normal fast pitch speed. The batters are not the only ones that time the pitcher's motions; so do the runners! That much extra time, EARLY in your windup, is enough for an eager base runner to come off the bag prematurely, before you release the ball, and, hopefully, early enough for an umpire to call them out.

This tactic not only has the desired effect on the batter's timing of the pitcher's motions but it will also control any base runner.

I have seen young pitchers use this tactic and get as many as seven base runners called for leaving early, in a single game. Using this tactic effectively can bring the most aggressive base-running teams to their knees and stop any attempts to steal.

Try this early in the game when you have a runner on base. You will get a few runners called out early in the game. After that they will be very cautious on the bags. They will delay coming off to avoid getting called out for leaving too soon. That extra moment of indecision on the part of the base runner will give your catcher extra time to pick them off even if they do decide to try. Don't use this in a game until you have a runner on the bags. The other team will be alerted that you are a smart pitcher. You will keep them glued to the bags and decrease their lead a step or two when you release the ball. Many times an unsuspecting team and coach will get several runners called out before they figure out what is happening and why.

Practice this tactic and remember it is important to bring the ball out of your glove as fast as if you were throwing a fastball. This makes you more unpredictable. Pull those runners off the bags and then control them with this tactic. Once you do use it in the game, use it three or four times every inning to keep them from challenging you as often.

Remember, on the fast-slow-fast variation, when you reach the slow section, your stride foot should hover a few inches above the rubber. Your body freezes for a second but your arm keeps moving. Then, when you speed it up again, continue your push off and stride and *STOMP ON THE GAS!*

There is also the slow-slow-fast, the slow-fast-slow and fast-fast-slow variations. Practice them all and have fun with them.

❹ *GLOVE DISTRACTIONS* This fourth step to become an unpredictable pitcher involves using your glove in your motions to distract the batter. Remember, you are allowed to hold the ball in presentation for up to 10 seconds. The hitters are waiting to see the ball come out of the glove. They want to see the ball and especially the grip. You are going to use this against them.

Once you have presented the ball at your waist for a single second, the requirements for bringing the hands together have been satisfied. What you do with your glove in the remaining nine seconds is up to you. As long as you keep the glove in front of you and don't separate your hands, you can move it around any way you choose.

Some tall pitchers like to present the ball, raise the glove high over their head, and come back down to their waist before starting their windup.

Some pitchers bring the glove up high and drop it down slowly in a jerky motion, as if coming down a ladder. They make four or five jerks as they bring it back down and as soon as they reach their waist, they start their windup. This tactic is called "The Fireman's Ladder."

Some pitchers move the glove around in circles across their stomach, as if they were rubbing their tummy, then separate the hands and go to the windup at some point in that motion. This is known as "The Tummy Rub."

Other pitchers bring the glove up high to the right, drop it low to the left, and then come straight across their waist, before going into their windup.

All of these are distraction tactics that utilize the pitcher's glove. What you do with your glove, as long as you do not separate your hands, can make you appear to be a completely different pitcher from the one that threw the last pitch. And, moving the glove around forces the batter to try harder to focus on the ball/grip once it comes out of the glove. Here is the kicker; when done quickly enough, you can start your windup while moving the glove in a different direction and the batter's eyes will follow the glove for a second or two, INSTEAD OF THE BALL!

Using the descriptions above, here are a few ideas to get you thinking. Bring the glove up over your head then back down to your waist. You don't have to wait until it comes ALL the way back down to your waist. You can remove the ball from the glove at any point and go directly into your forward windup, as long as you bring the ball out of the glove in a sideways motion.

If you bring it way up and drop it down in steps, you can bring the ball out of the glove on the third or fourth step instead of waiting until the last one at your waist. Start your windup on the last step for one pitch, and the third step on the second pitch, then the last, the second pitch, etc.

Bring the glove way up to the right, then way down to the left, then straight across your waist, then separate your hands and start your windup. Do that once or twice. Then, bring the glove way up to the right and bring the ball out, go into your windup at around the twelve o'clock position, while bringing the glove down to your left. It takes them by surprise and they will be watching the glove for a second.

If you make large, quick circles across your stomach, you can bring the ball out on the first circle, second, third, fourth, or whenever you choose. You can bring the ball into the windup and continue to make another part of a circle to draw them off even more. If you throw one or two pitches, bringing the ball out on the third circle, then throw one bringing it out on the first circle: SURPRISE!

You can make circles to the left for a few pitches and then to the right for a few. You can even make one circle to the left, two to the right, another to the left and then go into the windup, as long as you do it all inside that 10 seconds.

5 *UTILIZING THE LEG SLAP* Using the leg slap tactic during your normal pitching motion can distract the batter, but it can also work against you if you're not careful. If you do it consistently, the same way each time, the batter can use that noise to establish your pitching timing. That is *not* going to make you an unpredictable pitcher.

If you slap your leg, you *must* vary the timing. Don't do it at precisely the same moment every time. Practice intentionally slapping a little late and then a little early, compared to your customary timing. This will help confuse the batters and make you more unpredictable.

Think about these ideas. Feel free to come up with a few more. Use your imagination. There are countless styles to list here. Pitch smart. Always keep them guessing and have a blast!

CHAPTER FOURTEEN

DEALING WITH THE SLAP HITTER

Consider this: the batter before you presents a sacrifice bunt stance, causing the infield to move in closer and shift to cover. Suddenly, the batter pulls back into a normal stance and slaps at the ball hoping to drive it past the now too-close infielders. You have a "slapper" on your hands.

Alternately, the batter takes her stance at the back of the box. Then, just as you are about to release the ball, she charges forward and slaps the ball on the run. You have a "running slapper" on your hands.

One requirement for a slapper to make good contact and be successful is that they MUST time the pitch perfectly to ensure good, solid contact and to direct the ball where THEY want it to go.

If this happens to you frequently, it is because you have forgotten to implement the techniques I shared with you in the previous chapter to make you an unpredictable pitcher. Any attempt by the batters to slap hit off of you should be seen by you as a wakeup call. They're not just slapping the ball; they're slapping you!

YOU HAVE BECOME COMPLETELY PREDICTABLE.

The most effective method of combating this is to TAKE AWAY THE HITTER'S ABILITY TO TIME YOUR PITCH.

As we discussed in the previous chapter, there are ways a smart pitcher can prevent a batter from accurately timing her pitches. The best way is to change speeds from one pitch to the next. If you can practice and throw pitches at four different speeds (fast, slow and two somewhere in between) and you *constantly* change speeds from one pitch to the next, it is impossible for the batters to nail down your timing. Doing that is not only smart pitching against every batter; it makes it nearly impossible for a batter to execute a slap hit. They won't even try.

If you have fast pitches that are all within just a couple of miles per hour of each other, plus one slow change-up, throwing the change-up to a slapper can have the opposite effect to the one you desire. The slower speed gives the slapper more time to execute the slap hit. Instead, consider giving them a pitch much faster than they expect or are prepared to deal with.

You have heard me say this many times: batters at every level of play rely and depend on the pitcher's motions to decide when to swing. This is the biggest decision a batter makes. If they cannot use the pitcher's motions to help them, their decision time is cut back to approximately one-third of what they are used to. They do not perform well when rushed.

I'm going to share with you now one of the simplest of all delayed rotation pitching tactics covered in this book. It's called the "slow-fast" windup, and it's very effective against any batter, but particularly lethal against a slap hitter.

You begin with a nice, relaxed pitching motion. This somewhat slow motion implies that you are about to throw a very slow pitch, one that will barely reach the plate. (This is acting class now!) Then, as the ball reaches between the one and two o'clock positions in your windup, you speed up, throw fast and catch the batter off-guard with a pitch that is easily twice as fast as they anticipated.

Practice throwing your movement pitches with this delayed rotation tactic. You may very well discover that a few of those movement pitches break better than when thrown them from a normal full speed windup.

If you suspect a slapper, always go for the corners of the strike zone with a movement pitch. However, more important, *TAKE AWAY THEIR TIMING!*

Preventing batters from getting their timing down is a MAJOR part of any champion pitcher's game plan. Make it a part of your game plan and you will succeed.

CHAPTER FIFTEEN

A PITCHER'S PHILOSOPHY

If you talk to enough pitchers about their pitching, the game and their teams, you will find their philosophies vary a great deal.

What one pitcher regards as wisdom and knowledge, the next may discount as trivial. Usually the part of their pitching game that they do the best is the most important to them and they will stress it a great deal.

What others may consider to be a weak point will be dismissed as unimportant.

Over the years, I have talked with hundreds of fast pitch softball pitchers, team coaches, professional pitching coaches, and players to ascertain what makes up the best pitchers in the sport. It turns out that the best pitchers are not determined by their ball movement, speed, placing of the pitch or years of experience as a pitcher. The best and most widely respected pitchers are those who pitch the smartest games.

They don't have to throw the quickest fastball, or have a large number of different pitches to choose from, or even have great ball movement on those pitches. *The best pitchers are the unpredictable pitchers.* The unpredictable pitchers are the smart pitchers!

Years ago, my goal was to become a smart pitcher; to outsmart the batters, the teams I faced. Every good pitcher needs a bit of an ego when it comes to their pitching. I am no exception to this rule.

My pitching philosophy is different from any other I've encountered in the sport. Most do not even agree with me. But my philosophy is simple: a pitcher must be smarter at pitching than the batter is at hitting. That's pretty basic.

When I was fairly young, I figured out how important disrupting a hitter's timing was to a pitcher's game. I discovered that even the slightest delay in the batter's response time gave me a tremendous advantage. So I studied and developed pitching tactics and techniques to intimidate batters and delay their reaction time. Most pitchers don't give this much, if any, thought. I, however, gave it a lot of thought.

What I do know is that my philosophy earned me metro, regional and national ASA Men's "A" Division First Place championship trophies. I was voted the ASA's most valuable Men's "A" Division fast pitch softball pitcher in the nation. I won more tournaments and trophies than I can recall.

I am convinced that if I hadn't felt this way, very few of those victories would have been achieved. I felt that if my team did not win the first place trophies, we were losers. Not a terribly healthy attitude, especially for a kid just starting out. However, that was my driving force.

While most pitchers believe the only things they need to improve are ball speed, movement and placement of the pitch, I had a different philosophy. Sure, I worked on those areas as much as the next pitcher, but what set me apart was my goal to become the most dominating, controlling and feared pitcher that I could possibly be. I worked relentlessly to maintain unpredictability and a level of intimidation that would precede me at every tournament.

I used every legal tactic that I witnessed or invented. I focused on becoming totally unpredictable to the batters AND the runners. I differed every pitch from one inning to the next.

My philosophy was such that I was not content to simply throw a winning game. My ultimate goal was to deal the other team nothing less than a crushing defeat. That part of my philosophy was the driving force behind improving my game. I was aggressive and extremely intimidating. Every team dreamed of defeating me. I did my very best to destroy their dream and make playing against me a painful experience. I was definitely not Mr. Nice Guy in the rubber.

Many years have passed since then, and injuries prevent me from competing now in the position of this sport that I love so well, and I have retired from coaching. Now the time has come for me to pass on to a much wider audience what I have learned and coached all these years. I have nearly 50 years of experience being in and around fast pitch softball. These are some of the things that helped make me and my teams winners. I hope some of my advice can help you be a winner, too.

Here is the first piece of advice I always offer to anyone playing any sport: HAVE FUN!

CHAPTER SIXTEEN

THE WALL WORKOUT

Every pitcher thinks they require a catcher in order to practice. Well, I'm here to tell you that you don't need a catcher, a coach or even a softball park to practice your pitching.

Find a solid concrete or foundation brick wall—a handball court wall is ideal. Take a piece of chalk and draw a strike zone box on the wall. Make it the strike zone for your height. Then draw a line through the box, from left to right, at the same height as the belt on your waist. Draw it all the way across the strike zone box you chalked out. Measure off the same distance you use at your level of play, from the pitcher's rubber to home plate, and then subtract two feet. You want the distance to be where the ball would be struck by the batter, about one foot in front of the plate. Throw from there.

Work on accuracy first. You should be able to catch the returning ball without stepping left or right. An accurate throw will return straight back to you. Once you have become consistent at doing that, begin throwing harder. Remember, sacrificing accuracy for speed is NEVER a good idea. Accuracy comes first; *then* work on speed.

You don't need a pitching coach or an expensive radar gun to reveal if you are throwing harder than before. The harder you throw, the closer the ball will return to you without hitting the ground. If you can catch the ball without it hitting the ground, or without taking a step closer to the wall, it means you have fairly good speed for your level of play. As you progress, when you catch the ball, it will have more force behind it and you will be able to tell when you are throwing harder and faster.

Again, don't trade accuracy for speed. A 70 mph pitch is not impressive if you can't throw it for a strike. When you do the wall workout, take a portable radio/tape/CD unit along and play your favorite lively-paced music. Avoid playing slow tunes as that will slow down your workout pace. Try to throw for an hour every day after school. That's what I did.

"I couldn't find a catcher" is a poor excuse to avoid working out your pitching arm. As I said before, you don't need a catcher, a coach or a radar gun to work out, and discover if you're throwing harder and faster.

But we'll just keep that between you, me and the wall.

CHAPTER SEVENTEEN

PITCH SMART

If you read the rulebook, you'll see it says the pitcher must make a presentation. Well, they don't use that exact word anymore but it's still the same thing. You *must* present the ball for at least one second. You are *allowed* to present the ball for as long as ten seconds. And you must present the ball with your hands together in front of you.

You are also allowed to simply touch the side of the glove and simulate bringing the hands together. I want you to think about that for a moment. You take the call with the ball in your throwing hand, at your side, where everyone sees it. Then, at some point, you apply the grip to the ball. If you do not apply the grip to the ball inside the glove, guess what else everyone gets to see? Not bringing the hands together and applying the grip to the ball while it is inside the glove is not smart pitching.

HOWEVER, a smart pitcher will use every legal tool they can to be more effective at their position. The things you can do when you conceal the ball inside your glove can be awesome weapons in your arsenal of pitching tactics to control batters AND runners. If the call is for a drop ball, put that grip on the

ball at your side. Then, when the ball is in the glove, move that hand around like you are changing the grip. Then throw that drop! Or, if the call is for a drop, put a change-up grip on the ball at your side where everybody can see it. Then change the grip in the glove and throw the drop! See? You will be surprised how many players, coaches and even parents in the stands rely on reading the calls and watching for pitchers to give away the pitch, and relaying that to the batters.

The other team watches you warm up before the game and while you take your warm-up throws from the rubber. Once they feel they have your timing down in their heads, their confidence builds.

The batters are convinced they now know exactly when to pull the trigger and begin their swing. The base runners are confident as to exactly when to safely jump off the bag and take their lead. They have this confidence because **YOU GAVE IT TO THEM. YOU ARE PREDICTABLE** and that is not smart pitching.

A smart pitcher works very hard to stay unpredictable. The simplest way to stay unpredictable is to use the presentation as a tactic against the batters. You must present the ball for one second and you are allowed to present it for up to ten seconds. If you stagger, or vary, the amount of time you present the ball from one pitch to the next, you will throw their timing off and have an advantage over them.

Let's say you hold the ball in presentation for three seconds on the first pitch, and seven seconds on the next. That extra four seconds feels like an eternity to the batter after seeing that first pitch. They will hesitate and flinch; they will wonder what is going on. You have disrupted their concentration, giving you the advantage of surprise.

The same thing applies to the runners on the bags. They will hesitate, flinch, shift back and forth from one foot to the other and sometimes even jump off the bag too soon and get called out or not come off the bag at all because you have thrown off their timing and taken away their confidence. That is smart pitching.

You probably have heard the other team's coach yell something to his runners like, "I want you out there. Five steps, quick, jump off the bag". Wouldn't you rather hear him say, "Be smart. Stay awake. We need you there so don't leave too soon".

CHAPTER EIGHTEEN

THE ZONE IN THE ZONE

The zone in the zone. What the heck does that mean? Simple: inside the strike zone there is another zone.

This is an area inside the strike zone where you do not want to place the pitch. I have heard this zone called many things over the years: the meat locker, the tube, the pipe, the uh-uh zone and the oh-no zone, to name a few. Picture the strike zone as being a rectangle as wide as the plate and as high as any particular batter's strike zone would be. It will always be the same width but the height will vary with the height of each batter.

Picture those measurements and then envision another rectangle inside the first one. The second rectangle is one-third the width of the plate and one-third the height of that batter's strike zone. Now, picture that second rectangle being exactly in the center of the strike zone. *That inner zone is where you should avoid placing any pitch.*

This leaves one-third of the distance, all the way around the second zone, as the areas where you want to place the pitch. Let me explain.

When you throw a pitch inside the inner zone, the batter does not need to make a decision. They know that if they do not swing and make contact, that pitch will be called a strike. Unless they decide not to swing before the pitch is thrown, (0 & 3 count; something situational), there is about a ninety percent chance that they will swing. The batters will swing at that pitch simply because it is coming to the exact area where they want to see it, where they want it to be. The chance of their making good contact with the ball is much greater when it is heading for the inner zone.

When you throw at the outer edges of the zone instead of the inner zone, the batter must make a decision whether to swing at that pitch or not. That decision takes time. The batter must hesitate and flip a coin in her head to make that decision because there isn't sufficient time to think it through. "Is the ump going to call this a strike or a ball?" she wonders. Some batters can make this decision almost instantly; others can't, even by the time the ball crosses the plate for a strike. Every batter hopes the ump calls any pitch they don't swing at a ball.

The batters have a desire to let a pitch go by for a ball. That's another way for them to show their skill at batting, and drawing a walk takes the pressure off them to get a hit. This is a weakness that can be used against them. You can make them hesitate when deciding whether they should swing at the pitch or cross their fingers and hope it's called for a ball. There is a reason for throwing at the outer edges of the strike zone. Sneaky and smart!

You want the batter to think it is a ball but the umpire to see it as a strike. You also want the batter to think it's a strike when the umpire sees it as a ball. You will get more strike calls and missed swings when you throw balls that look like strikes and strikes that look like balls.

Throw to the outer edges of the strike zone, and stay out of the zone in the zone. My favorite pitch has always been a called third strike that was not swung on. Make it yours, too.

CHAPTER NINETEEN

DEALING WITH THE BUNT

You are in the circle. You take the call. You start to present the ball and the batter turns in the box to bunt.

How do you make bunting as difficult as possible for the batter?

Simple. Four words: **FAST, HIGH AND INSIDE**.

When the batter turns to bunt, they place the part of the bat that they want to make contact with the ball directly over the plate. Many times their hand is behind the bat at the same point or very near it. That will place their hand, a part or all of their arm, and sometimes even their shoulder, in the strike zone or the area between the plate and the box.

The batter is concerned with getting a hit. You want to make her forget about getting a hit and worry more about getting hit. If the ball hits any part of the batter's body that is over the strike zone, it is a strike.

You may have to risk confusing your catcher when this happens. You may have to throw a different pitch instead of whatever was called for, without her realizing. Even if you have to hold the ball in presentation for an extra second or two, change your target from the catcher's glove to the area of the bat that is just inside of the batter's hand closest to the plate.

The batter will instinctively pull back, raise the bat and knock themselves slightly off balance. They'll inadvertently take a step or half-step in the direction opposite to where they want to go, (assuming here that it's a right-handed batter). The batter will pull away from the plate and, in almost every case, the bat will be coming up at the same time. If your pitch is high and inside, you stand a better than average chance of getting a foul tip off the bat as they fall backwards.

They may be quick enough to get out of the way. They may foul tip it off their bat, or take it on their fingers for a strike. Either way, your chances of getting a strike and preventing a bunt are better than average.

If you add this to your offensive pitching tactics, be sure to discuss it with your catcher before the game. Fast, high and inside will alter any batter's plans to bunt the ball into play.

CHAPTER TWENTY

YOUR INTIMIDATION FACTOR

Eye contact or none at all. Spitting on the ground and where. The look on your face, your general attitude on the rubber and what the other team thinks of you when you are on the rubber. This and more add up to create your intimidation factor. Off the playing field, it's admirable to be the nicest person that anyone could ever want to meet. But on the field? No. Carrying that nice person reputation into the circle can cost you the win.

If you have ever stepped into the batter's box against a champion pitcher, one who is always in control, you know the feeling you have for them. You want to get a hit so bad off of her you can taste it. If you get that hit it makes your whole month and you know why. Because if you do not, you know you were just another notch on her gun, just another statistic in the book and not one iota more.

You picked up your weapon, stepped into the box, declared war and lost the battle. When the smoke cleared, you were the loser and she treated you as such. She gave you the feeling she was disgusted at your very appearance on the same field and insulted that you thought you might be good enough to make contact with any pitch she threw.

That pitcher gave you the feeling that she didn't care if you existed at all; you meant nothing to her. You were just one in a long line of victims, just another 'K' in the scorebook. She never even looked at your face until she struck you out. Then you glimpsed her smirk.

Surely she knew you were there, right in front of her. She did spit in your direction right before she threw that second strike.

The most irritating part about it all, you knew that was more than likely going to happen before you even picked up the bat.

That pitcher's intimidation factor helped her win the battle against you. It will be even easier for her to win the battle the next time. The next time you will want a hit even more than this time. She will use that against you too, because that is the kind of pitcher she is.

She almost never talks to anyone on the opposing team before the game. When she does, it is usually to rub salt in their wound recalling the last tournament they played in when she struck them out.

Before and during the game, you don't like her at all. You would like nothing better than to drive one of her pitches right back into her gut. You are also reasonably certain that is exactly what she wants to do to you when you are in the box facing her.

You recall that one tournament when a batter crowded the plate and caught a high inside fastball in the jaw. She got knocked out cold and did the funky chicken on the ground. You remember that the pitcher showed absolutely no remorse and even appeared angry on the mound. She demanded the ball back immediately, like she wanted the next victim in the lineup to step forward.

After the game you heard her say, "Why should I feel sorry for her? She knows how hard I throw. I didn't mean to hit her. She gets a free trip to first base because she was either too stupid to know when to move or too slow to get out of the way. I'm the one people should feel sorry for. I got robbed of a strikeout."

You also remember that one time you made the mistake of trying to bunt on her, how she seemed to change her target, in mid-windup, from the catcher's glove to the fingers on your left hand. You remember the bruise on your ribcage and that they called it a strike because it hit your fingers before it hit your ribs. You also remember she made no showing of emotion then either.

You remember your second baseman striking out and coming into the dugout, her face red as a beet she was so mad. She said the pitcher had brushed her back and almost hit her; she did it intentionally because right before she threw the next pitch, the pitcher shot her a quick smile. Then you remind the second baseman of the bruise on your ribs and how you could hardly swing a bat for a week because of your fingers. Then you both notice the on-deck batter, the new kid on the team, staring at you with her eyes as big as hubcaps.

Congratulations. The new kid has never seen this pitcher before and the pitcher has never seen her either but the kid is already intimidated because that's how it works for a champion pitcher.

That kind of intimidation cannot be bought. It must be earned, and maintained once acquired. When that pitcher is on the rubber she commands one hundred percent of everyone's attention one hundred percent of the time. When she walks into the park, within a few minutes, everyone knows she has arrived. Her presence in the park is felt.

There are literally hundreds of ways to intimidate the other team members—far too many to spell them all out.

Here are some of my all-time favorite intimidation tactics:

1. You are on the rubber and take the call. Hold the ball in your presentation in front of you long enough for the batter to call time and step out of the box. You can hold it there for up to 10 seconds but the batter will normally step out at around seven or eight seconds. When the batter steps out, freeze like a statue, keep both feet on the rubber and keep the ball inside your glove. Do not look at the batter or the umpire; stay frozen and stare at your catcher's mask. Have no expression on your face at all. Stay in your stance, ready to throw. When the batter

steps back in and the ump signals to play ball, stay frozen for another four or five seconds. Then step back off the rubber, call time and retie one of your shoelaces. By doing this you send the message to the other team that it does not matter to you what they do. They can call time, step out, dance a jig, or set off a bomb. Nothing they can do will have the slightest effect whatsoever on what YOU are about to do to them.

2. You have just thrown a called strike against a batter. You get the ball back and put both feet on the rubber. As you are getting the call sign from the catcher, break out in a grin and start chuckling. Don't laugh out loud; just chuckle so it's noticeable. The batter will probably call time. If not, you call time and turn away from the batter but keep chuckling so she sees you doing it. Signal for your catcher to come to you and meet her halfway. Whisper to your catcher that you are just trying to annoy the batter. The batter will already be unhappy thinking you were laughing at her. When you throw the next strike, laugh out loud for a few seconds. The third strike is guaranteed.

3. Now, if you are up to this, who is the easiest batter on the other team for a pitcher to intimidate? Whichever batter is in the ON-DECK CIRCLE! You take the call, present the ball in front of you and then slowly turn your head and look at the on-deck batter. Smile at her, wipe the smile off your face, and THEN turn your head back to the batter and throw your pitch.

Use your imagination, stay unpredictable, and mess with your opponents' heads every way you can. It's OK to gently give their ability a little insult now and then. It can be a lot of fun too.

CHAPTER TWENTY-ONE

THE FAKEOUT PICK-OFF PLAY

I am going to add this in as a pitching tactic, although your catcher will do almost all the work on this one.

There is a runner on third base. The pitcher throws a pitch. The catcher pops up and looks at that runner who is now three to four steps off the bag. The runner is staring back and watching the catcher like a hawk. The catcher draws back, the runner sees this and moves back closer to third base. Now there is no play because the runner is too close to the bag for the catcher to pick her off.

During any given game, 95% of the eyes will be on the ball, or on the person who is in control of the ball at that instant. In the case of the base runners, it's more like 99%. When a pitch is thrown, the base runners watch the catcher's every movement, no matter how slight.

Now, I am addressing this to the catchers. When you come up with the ball and look the runner back, you are facing them. You are an immediate threat to them because you have the ball. The instant you draw your arm back when you are facing them, they move back to safety. When you are not facing them, you are still a threat because you have the ball, however, you are not perceived as being as big a threat as when you *are* facing them. You can use this knowledge to your advantage to fool the third base runner and pick them off before they can get back to the bag.

This is a tactic that requires the catcher have a good and accurate throwing arm. It will take practice to master but it is definitely worth the time and effort. Note: younger catchers may not be able to do this particular move.

Here is the play. The pitcher throws the ball. The catcher stands up, takes a quick glance at third base and sees the runner is off the bag by three or four steps. The third baseman is at the bag ready to catch any throw you make. You turn your head back towards your pitcher, take two steps forward and draw back as if you are going to give a lazy throw back to the pitcher. However, instead of throwing the ball to the pitcher, you keep facing the pitcher and throw the ball across the front of your body sidearm to the third baseman without looking directly at third base. You turn towards third base *as* you are throwing the ball, *as you are spinning*. AHA! Now you see why this must be practiced until perfect before attempting it in a game.

The runner will expect you to throw the ball to the pitcher because you are facing that direction. You don't turn towards third base until you are making the throw. The runner has no forewarning until the throw is made. The ball will be in the hands of the third baseman before the runner realizes they are in trouble.

Sneaky Softball Pitching

It is very important you take the two easy steps forward so you will not be throwing straight down the baseline and hit the runner. Moving forward two steps lets you throw clear of the runner on the base line.

Admittedly, this tactic is risky. It takes practice, and not every catcher, especially the very young ones, will be able to master this. Occasionally, if the throw is not precise, you will hit the runner with the ball or it could go wild. There will be no back up signal unless you work one out to alert your fielders.

Your third baseman should be prepared to receive a surprise throw from you at any time there is a runner on third. The same goes for your first baseman, as this can be applied in the same manner there.

When you make this throw, you as the pitcher must then move to cover home plate in case of a run down on the base line.

If you do not have some type of signal, the remaining fielders will be just as surprised by that throw as that third base runner. It will take a moment for them to position themselves to back you up. You won't be able to throw the ball as fast as when you face your target, however, the element of surprise will definitely be on your side. You will also be surprised at how many runners you can pick off like this, at both the third and first bases.

Remember, a threat is, for the most part, perception. The size of the threat is what the person being threatened takes it to be. A base runner will perceive the catcher to be a smaller threat if the catcher is not facing that base runner.

If you cannot throw the ball sidearm, across the front of your body, accurately or with enough force to reach third base, you can still have the advantage of surprise. Size, strength and experience will prohibit many younger catchers from using this tactic as I have described. Here is what I suggest for those younger catchers:

Instead of throwing sidearm across the front of your body, shift all your weight to your left foot, pivot, spin and throw straight ahead towards third base. You will have to make this move very quickly with no hesitation at all. It will place you off balance; you may have to catch yourself from falling.

CHAPTER TWENTY-TWO

THE CLOTHESLINE AND BLANKET CHANGE-UP—THE KILLER CHANGE

Back when I was about 13 years old, we had a clothesline strung along the side of our house. One day my mother had hung an old blanket on the clothesline. At the time, I was at the side of the house practicing my pitching against a foundation block wall at the corner of the yard near the clothesline. I turned and threw a pitch into the blanket. (I admit I had a bit of an ornery streak). Immediately, Mom hollered at me from the kitchen window. I hadn't noticed she was there doing dishes and looking out right at me. She yelled at me again to not throw at the blanket or I'd be in big trouble.

I walked up to within one step of the blanket as if to throw a fastball into it, however, I stopped my hand right before the ball touched the blanket. Mom hollered at me while I was in my windup. I held the ball out to show her it was still in my hand. My mother gave me a look as if to say, "OK, you fooled me on that one but don't do it again!"

I stopped and thought for a moment. She was convinced I had let go with a fastball into that blanket because that's what my motions (my windup) made her think. I wondered how well that tactic might work against a batter in the box. So I began practicing, pretending the blanket was in front of me. I made the windup look like a fastball until the ball was almost to my hip. Then I abruptly slowed my arm speed and released the ball just ahead of my front leg at the hip. I practiced for 15 minutes or so, to where I could show a fastball windup but release the ball so slowly that it barely reached the wall. I felt a quiver of excitement. I knew I had hit on a potentially powerful weapon.

I asked my mother to come outside and had her stand by the wall. I told her I was working on a change-up pitch and wanted her opinion. (Mom had been the scorekeeper for my dad's team for several years and had seen several hundred pitchers in their games and tournaments.)

What I did not tell my Mom was that I had a plastic Wiffle ball in my glove instead of a real softball.

Mom stood off to the side to watch. As I began my motion, I turned slightly to face her and threw my "clothesline and blanket" change-up directly at her.

Mom screamed and threw her hands up in front of her. The Wiffle ball barely reached her, bouncing gently off her hip. She was so startled, her hands were shaking. I apologized and, once she recovered, she said it was the scariest change-up she had ever seen.

When my Dad came home from work later that day, I asked him come outside with his glove. I said I'd been working on a new pitch and wanted his opinion. I repeated the clothesline and blanket pitch, this time with a real softball. The first one I threw stunned him so much he didn't even close

the glove on the ball when it hit. The ball fell to the ground and he stared at it, his mouth wide open. After several more, he said it was the best change-up he had ever seen in the all the years he had been playing fast pitch.

He asked how I gripped the ball. I showed him my fastball grip. He said most pitchers have a particular grip they use when throwing a slow change-up. His team members knew the grips to watch for and many times knew when a change-up was coming early in the pitcher's windup. Mine, however, he said, did not reveal itself that way. Dad saw my fastball grip and thought that a fastball was being thrown.

I used that change-up very successfully throughout my career. Now that I've given you its history, let me tell you how I teach it to the young pitchers I've worked with.

I have them throw three or four fastballs while I am standing to the throwing side and just ahead of them as they pitch. I watch very closely and determine EXACTLY at what point in front of them they open their hand and release the ball. Then I hold my glove out in the way of the pitch a few inches closer to them than that release point.

Then I ask them to show me a fastball windup but instruct them to slow the ball down just as it nears the hip, and to stop the ball just before it touches my glove. I point out how, when riding their bicycles, they know the difference between "touching the brakes" and "slamming on the brakes." I say I want them not to slam on the brakes when slowing down the ball but merely touch the brakes, and stop the hand just before it touches the glove. I tell them they are students in an acting class, and I am going to teach them to act in a way to fool the batters. I want them to convince the batters they are going to get the fastest pitch possible, and then fool them with a real slow one instead. This is called "selling the pitch," when it comes to throwing a slow change-up.

We practice using a fastball windup, stopping the ball before it hits the glove. I pay close attention to precisely where the student begins slowing down the ball. It typically takes several tries to prolong the fast windup to the point where the ball is almost to the hip. Initially it will visibly slow down behind them during the downswing.

Once they develop the deceptive fast windup and stop the ball at the glove, I take the glove away and tell them to pretend the glove is still there. This time when they stop their hand, I want them to open it and just let go of the ball. I tell them to make sure they do not use any follow-through after release; instead, pretend the glove is still there in the way. They are amazed to see the ball reach the plate when they do this.

It will not take much practice to control the location as they are using their familiar fastball grip. It will not take much more practice to release the ball at a speed between fast and slow, an off-speed pitch, again using their familiar fastball grip.

Batters rely upon watching the pitcher's motion, especially their arm speed, to determine how fast the ball is coming toward them. This tells them when to pull the trigger and start their swing. That is an advantage for the batters *IF* the pitcher allows them that advantage. TAKE THAT ADVANTAGE AWAY FROM THE BATTERS and they will have no choice but to watch the ball travel from the pitcher's hand partway to the plate before realizing how fast or slow the ball is approaching on this change-up pitch. AND THAT IS TIME THEY HAVEN'T GOT!

Make it as difficult as you can for batters to time your pitches. Change speeds constantly and watch how poorly even the best hitters will perform.

On a side note, make sure your pitcher does not throw with the arm straight and the elbow locked as this is very stressful to the female shoulder complex. Pitching with the elbow locked effectively locks out the large muscles of the upper arm and places virtually the entire load onto the shoulder muscles. Keep a tiny bend in the elbow throughout the entire arm circle to avoid this.

CHAPTER TWENTY-THREE

LEARNING TO THROW OFF-SPEED

If a pitcher throws every pitch at the same speed, no matter how fast that is, she'll get pounded by the third inning. Batters rely and depend on timing the pitcher's motions to make that big decision - when to pull the trigger and start their swing. To be a successful pitcher, you must take that advantage away from the batters.

Mastering off-speed pitching is a tactic all by itself. Many pitchers will throw one certain pitch for a single off-speed pitch, using a particular grip, and no more. Hitters are taught to look for the grips to judge what pitch is coming, including change-up grips. It is far more effective to throw all of your different pitches at different speeds, from one pitch to the next.

Let's take the fastest pitch—the pitch you throw faster than any other. That same fast pitch, that same grip, can be thrown at, say, 55, 45 and 40 mph. Now your one single fast pitch can be disguised to look like three different pitches. You do not need a separate grip for a slow or off-speed pitch.

That same fast pitch, thrown at a different speed, from one pitch to the next, forces the batter to guess when to start her swing.

This is the simplest way I have found to train a pitcher to throw one pitch at different speeds (an off-speed pitch). It requires nothing more than a solid concrete wall, a piece of chalk and a tape measure.

Find a concrete or foundation brick wall (preferably with no windows!) A handball court wall is ideal. DO NOT USE A STUCCO WALL - a stucco wall is only around one inch thick and can be damaged.

Draw a strike zone on the wall with chalk, the strike zone representing the pitcher's height. Now draw a line across the box dividing the zone into top and bottom halves. For this drill, the pitcher should only throw to the top half of the zone.

Have the pitcher throw at the top half of the zone at 100 percent full speed. Have her keep throwing and backing up to the point the ball just reaches her without hitting the ground. Draw a line on the ground where she starts that pitch. Now we have established the 100 percent mark.

Next, measure the distance from the wall to the point of what would be the regulation throwing distance for the pitcher's level of play, and then subtract two feet from that length. Draw a line at that point. The distance from the rubber to where the batter would hit the ball should be about two feet in front of the back tip of home plate. Now, have the pitcher throw her slowest change-up several times and draw a line at an average distance where the ball comes back and hits the ground. Now you have established the 40 percent mark. (The percentage is not exact; I am using this as an estimate).

Now, measure the distance between the 40 percent mark and the 100 percent mark. Divide that distance into three equal parts and draw a line at what would be the 60 percent and 80 percent distances. Now have the pitcher return to the 100 percent mark and throw from there.

Have the pitcher throw her fast ball, the pitch she throws with her fast ball grip. Have the pitcher gently put on the brakes at the end of the windup so the ball only returns as far as the 60 percent mark. Have her practice that until she can consistently throw it to where the ball comes off the wall and lands on, or very near, the 60 percent line. It will not take long for her to figure this out, as she will catch on to this quickly. It is important to continue keeping the windup at 100 percent full speed, but gently slow it down at the last moment.

Once she is consistent at 60 percent, have her do the same thing and have the ball return to the 80 percent mark by again applying the brakes to the last bit of the windup. Have her practice throwing at that speed until she can consistently come down on, or very near, the 80 percent line.

Then have her throw to the different lines on command. Have her throw a pitch at 100 percent, then 60 percent, 100 percent, 80 percent, 80 percent, 60 percent, 60 percent, 100 percent, 60 percent, etc. Once she can do this and come pretty close to the correct speed/line, she is ready to try it on the batters.

When one pitch is a different rate of speed then the previous pitch—and there are seldom two pitches in a row the same speed–the batters have greater difficulty deciding when to swing. They will have to depend on watching the ball travel from the pitcher's hand to determine exactly how fast it is coming. Forcing them to do that reduces the amount of time they have available to around 40 percent.

You can also divide the distance between the 40 percent and 100 percent lines into two equal parts and establish 40 percent, 70 percent and 100 percent distances. This will give the pitcher two speeds available for any particular pitch. The 100 percent distance will be accurate; the others are estimated.

Sneaky Softball Pitching

CHAPTER TWENTY-FOUR

THE BATTER/PITCHER THING

If you ever played softball, or even baseball for that matter, you know that something happens between the pitcher and the batter. There is a certain "thing" that happens. It's a head thing, a mental thing, a psychological thing. If a young pitcher does not recognize it and understand it, it can have a very dramatic effect on their performance. It seldom helps the pitcher. It is a completely separate battle unto itself. It is a mental battle and the pitcher must win.

The batter step up to the batter's box. She takes a few vicious swings. She steps in, digs in, tightens up all her muscles and takes her stance. She has just wasted everyone's time by extending that part of the batting ceremony as tediously long as possible. It does nothing but delay the game a few more seconds and bore everyone to death. Doing that doesn't even benefit the batter. It has absolutely no influence on her performance.

Once the batter has gotten that far, she is ready to do the most important mental thing she can do while in the box.

She turns her head to look directly at the pitcher's face; she seeks eye contact. She tries to initiate the batter / pitcher "thing." She gives you her most determined, fierce, intimidating, ugly look she can muster. She wants you to see her face—especially her eyes. She NEEDS you to see her eyes, she NEEDS eye contact—she needs feedback and she needs it badly.

This is how she determines how confident the pitcher is and, believe me, she'll see it right there in the pitcher's eyes as she looks at the batter.

Once you do that, once you look directly into the batter's eyes, make any eye contact at all, no matter how brief, you have just lost that first battle between pitcher and batter. Make no mistake; this is a battle. Not a battle of physical strength and ability, but one of wits—a mental battle. With every pitcher and batter, there is one winner here and one loser. Either you win or you lose; there is no gray area here. And it all happens before a single pitch is thrown or the bat is swung.

Why is eye contact with the pitcher so important to a batter? Let me explain.

Let's say you are walking down the hallway at school. You see someone you know walking towards you. You watch them as they get closer, waiting in anticipation for at least a smile and nod, if not to stop and chat, something that acknowledges you as a person who matters to them. You watch in stunned disbelief when that person walks right past you without so much as a glance. Disbelief turns to anger. You feel outraged at being completely ignored. "What's wrong with them?" you wonder. "How can they pretend like I don't even exist?" It upset you a little, maybe even a lot. It's all you can think about now. Your mind keeps returning to it throughout the day. You are distracted.

That is what you want to create in the mind of the batter when they are in the box. The batter is you walking down that hallway. And you are about to snub them.

You avoid eye contact. You want the batter feel slighted, unnoticed, insignificant, unimportant—not worth seeing. You want her to feel so unworthy of your notice that she will get upset. You want to ruin her day.

You need to demonstrate how worthless their time in the batter's box is to you and your team. She's wasting *your* time. You want them to dread the time she encounters you.

As I've said before, off the field, by all means be the nicest person anyone could hope to meet. You should be. But while you are in that circle, you are at war. You must drop that nice person image and *you must make sure the other team knows it.*

No matter what you might think, how cocky you think you look, don't do it. Once you make eye contact with the batter, the batter wins. It's that simple. Remember, there is no gray area in this first contest.

You look at the batter, you lose. You ignore the batter, you win.

If you make eye contact briefly, the batter will interpret that as fear. If you make eye contact for too long, the batter will interpret it as your lack of confidence in yourself and your ability.

In either case, if you make eye contact, the batter wins that first battle because now *you have given the batter confidence.* The batter is convinced that you are either scared of them or doubt your own ability, or both. They will be more aggressive and more daring when they swing the bat because you have given them that confidence. You handed them that slight edge all because you made eye contact.

You could have controlled them but you chose to look into their eyes. When you control the ball, you control the game, and the pitcher controls the ball more often than any other single player on the team. How you exercise that control will determine how effective you are as a pitcher.

I know what you're thinking—what about the intimidation factor we talked about back in chapter 20? How can I do that if I'm not permitted to look the batter in the eye? Yes, in certain circumstances it DOES benefit the pitcher to make eye contact with a particular batter. It is an intimidation tactic and you must make absolutely certain how it is presented. There can be no doubt in the batter's mind at all, or it will work against you. It must be accompanied with a very insulting grin and it must be timed and presented so the batter immediately steps out of the box for fear you might hit them with the next

pitch. If you do this and the batter does not step out of the box, your attempt to intimidate has failed. Instead, you just made yourself appear nervous and afraid. And you're now facing a very confident and much more aggressive batter. See what I mean?

Young pitchers likely won't understand the psychology of this. They see it nothing more than a "stare down." They think the pitcher and the batter are supposed to give each other dirty looks. It's crucial that you develop this in a young pitcher.

I have seen some young pitchers suffer from this psychological warfare. Some had trembling spells during the game, some got sick to their stomachs, some got so tense they had difficulty breathing. Sadly, this can sometimes result in the young pitcher quitting the sport all together.

Often it is attributed to nerves or immaturity. It is seldom recognized for what it really is: nothing more than one kid looking into the eyes of another kid. That other kid looks back at the kid holding the ball as if she hates that kid's guts. For a child, naturally seeking approval and acceptance, that can have a deep psychological effect that will invariably be explained away with some vague and incorrect generalization.

Just be aware this can happen. It happens more often than you might think. Any kid receiving that many dirty looks from a number of kids is going to be bothered by it to some extent. Sometimes, depending on the particular kid, it can bother them a great deal.

To be a winning pitcher, you must understand that there are only four people on the field—the pitcher, the catcher, the umpire and *the next strike-out victim*. That person is nameless. That person is faceless. They are nothing more than a statistic in a book. If you see them as be anything more than that, they will negatively affect your mental state while you are pitching.

Get in the habit of staring at your catcher's facemask and look *only* at that. You might be very surprised at how hard and to what extent the batters will try to get the pitcher to make eye contact with them. Now they are thinking about the pitcher instead of the ball. When that happens, guess who wins? *YOU do!*

Here's a little secret I want you to think about. I will not go into great detail, I want you to figure this one out.

Of all the batters on the other team, which one is the easiest for the pitcher to intimidate? Answer; whatever batter is in THE ON DECK CIRCLE!

CHAPTER TWENTY-FIVE

CRUD HAPPENS

This is not a tactic per se, however, it is such an important thing for young pitchers to understand that I feel compelled to include it.

Let's say you take your bicycle out and ride down the street. Suddenly you run over something you hadn't noticed. You turn your head around, look behind you and see that you just went through some dog's business card.

Do you keep looking behind you and focus on what you just ran over, or do you turn your head back forward again, so you don't go through more of the same? In that respect, pitching is like riding a bicycle.

Anyone that rides a bike, while they are looking backwards, will run into all kinds of crud. It's bound to happen.

A pitcher makes a throw they feel was a strike, however, the umpire calls it a ball. The pitcher gets unhappy with the umpire or themselves. Now the pitcher is looking back and thinking about the last pitch, when they should be focusing on the next pitch. The last pitch did not turn out as the pitcher hoped it would. That pitch was crud.

If you throw a pitch that doesn't work out like you would like it to, shake it off. FORGET ABOUT IT! It is already in the past. NOTHING is going to change. The call was made and cannot be appealed. What's done is done. *FORGET ABOUT IT.*

Don't think about it, don't worry about it and *don't let it affect the rest of your game.*

Focus on your next throw because you CAN do something about that one. Stay focused on what is ahead: the next pitch. You still have a say in what you are ABOUT to do.

If you dwell on the crud, that same crud will more than likely cause you to go through more crud, and more and more. How many times have you seen a pitcher get upset about something and never recover, even if they finish the rest of the game. That one single pitch, that one single call, takes them completely out of the inning and sometimes the entire game. Don't be that pitcher.

With every single pitch you throw, once it is done, it is a new ball game with a new challenge.

Crud happens. It happens to every one of us. It has always happened and it will happen again. The best way to avoid running into a lot of it is to keep your focus straight ahead on what is still to come.

Only when you look ahead can you see your target and hit it. The chances of you hitting a target that is behind you are slim to none. The past is over; the future lies ahead. You cannot focus on the past without turning your back on the future.

Nothing gives the other team greater pleasure than to see the opposing pitcher lose her focus and composure. Nothing builds the other team's confidence and aggressiveness like it either. It's a huge advantage and it ALWAYS helps the other team.

If you do focus on the crud that just happened and get upset about it, don't worry. You still might win the Most Valuable Player trophy. The Most Valuable Player of the *OTHER* team!

CHAPTER TWENTY-SIX

YOUR PITCHING FACE

This tactic falls into the mental part of the game and can have a very positive effect on a pitcher.

Many young pitchers inadvertently give away how fast the next pitch is coming. No matter how hard they try to hide the ball and protect the call, the look on their face gives that part of the pitch away to the batter. Their face can be like a billboard when it comes to the speed of the pitch they are about to throw. That fact is being used against you, the pitcher. You need to turn it around and use it against the hitters.

When a pitcher is about to cut loose with a fast throw, the look on her face as she goes through her windup will, be one of great strain. Their face will contort and every muscle on it will flex in preparation for a tremendous effort. You would think they were pushing a car uphill!

That same pitcher will have a more relaxed look on her face when she is about to throw a slower pitch. Again, her face reads like a billboard and gives away the speed of the pitch.

Many pitchers will throw with a very sullen expression or no expression at all. Those pitchers do not give away the pitch but they fail to use the look on their face as a tactic to their advantage.

If you normally do not have any expression on your face when you throw, try using a look of great strain when you throw an off-speed pitch or a slow change-up. Then, the next time you use that look of great strain, throw a fast one by the batter. Then, on the next pitch, use that same look of great strain, add a well-timed, loud grunt at the release and throw another slow one. Then throw a fast one with a very relaxed look on your face.

Use the look on your face to your advantage. You will be surprised how much the batters notice it and how easy it is to throw them off doing this.

CHAPTER TWENTY-SEVEN

TEACHING THE DELAYED ROTATION PITCHES

Picture the forward rotation of your arm during the windup.

The rulebook says once you separate your hands, (remove the ball from the glove while in presentation) and start your forward rotation, it may not be stopped or reversed. It also says that once you release the ball for delivery, you cannot make another forward revolution.

It does not say at what speed it must be done or that any one part of it can't be faster or slower than any other part. We are going to use that to our advantage.

Again, picture the forward rotation of your arm in the windup. Now, we are going to divide the windup into three separate stages:

The stage where you separate the ball from the glove, to the point where the ball is brought up in front of you (the ball is about as high as your shoulder).

The stage where the ball is about as high as your shoulder, to the point the ball has just passed directly overhead.

The stage where the ball has just passed overhead, to the end of your windup, where you open your hand to release the ball for delivery.

Now step back and go through each of these three stages of the motion one at a time, VERY SLOWLY. Pause slightly between each stage and count out "One, two, three", as you execute each of the three stages. Do this a few times. We are pausing between the three stages so your brain, arm and muscles will recognize the stages as being separate. You obviously would not hesitate like this during a game, (besides, it's not legal), but this exercise is necessary to help your body understand the delineation between these three stages.

We will call the rotation you just did SLOW/SLOW/SLOW.

Now, a slow change-up is nothing more than a FAST/FAST/SLOW windup, if we look at it and describe it in this way.

Now, we are going to try a FAST/SLOW/FAST windup using the same three stages as before. However, this time we will not pause between the three stages and, instead, let one part flow into the next. When you do this, say out loud, "Fast, slooooow, fast", as you execute each stage. Remember not to pause between the stages now. Make the SLOW stage take between three-quarters of a second to one full second.

Make the first stage appear as if you are going to throw a fastball, slow down for stage two, then speed up stage three and deliver a good off-speed pitch at around 80% of your fastest speed.

Just 15 minutes practicing this and you will find the batters hesitating, jerking, shifting their weight to the rear foot WAY too soon, and even holding their front foot in the air trying to catch themselves.

Doing this technique takes away the majority of a batter's ability to determine exactly when to begin their swing. A lot of the time they will not swing at all because they cannot decide when to start their swing in time.

Another added benefit of the FAST/SLOW/FAST windup is this; the tactic gives any antsy runners on the bags enough time, in the first stage of the windup, to come off the bags too soon and get called out. The runners are timing the pitcher's motions just as the batters do, and they, too, will make mistakes.

Use this about every third or fourth pitch. The batters will never be sure exactly when to begin their swing.

Here are some combinations. You likely already do a FAST/FAST/SLOW windup for your slow change-up. But did you know you can also use SLOW/FAST/SLOW for a different type of change-up?

SLOW/SLOW/FAST is an awesome combination for an off-speed pitch.

SLOW/FAST/SLOW is also good but takes a little more practice to perfect the timing.

Keep the FAST stages FAST, the SLOW stages SLOW and *do not* use MEDIUM anywhere in the formula for these tactics.

A medium pace anywhere in the windup will give the batters time to adjust to the delivery speed. Watch closely and make sure the FASTs and SLOWs are not blended into one long MEDIUM-paced motion.

I have taught this to 10- and 12-year-olds in a mere 15 minutes before a game. They have gone into their games and gotten more strikeouts on average, with as many as five runners additionally called out for leaving the bags too soon. I have also taught it to several college pitchers who experienced similar improvements.

Remember, do not stop the rotation in between the three stages.

Be sure, when you do the FAST-SLOW-FAST, when you get to the SLOW stage, your stride foot should be hovering above the ground by a few inches. When you speed up to FAST, continue with your push-off and stride. Your body freezes for a second but your arm keeps moving. Many pitchers fail to lift that stride foot. It is important that you lift your foot as that also sells the pitch.

It may be a good idea to have your coach speak with the plate umpire just before the game but out of earshot of the other team coach. Let the umpire know that you will occasionally throw with an arm

motion that has more than one speed, that parts of it vary between fast and slow. It's good to make them aware so they are not taken by surprise just like the batters. They will probably reply that it's OK as long as she does not stop or reverse it. They'll be prepared and not distracted by it.

Practice these exercises in front of a mirror empty-handed. *Don't be tempted to hold a ball doing this exercise.*

Fine-tuning your technique (Arm circle points for speed changes in delayed rotation pitches):

SLOW-FAST: Speed up your arm EXACTLY at the two o'clock position. Begin as if you are throwing a pitch that will barely reach the catcher. Then, at two o'clock, speed up, throw hard and finish with a fast stride. It won't be quite as long as a normal leap and drag stride but you can still get a little push off the rubber if you want to.

FAST-SLOW: Slow down halfway between the five and six o'clock positions, just before reaching the hip. Use the customary motions, speed, push-off and stride length of your fastest pitch. Tap the brakes on your arm motion as your arm nears the hip before release. Please note I did not say SLAM on the brakes: I said TAP. With just a little practice you can develop several delivery speeds for an assortment of off-speed pitches that will all appear to be fastballs to the batters. Having control of three speeds is a major tactic in itself and few batters can deal with that effectively. For even better results, develop four or more speeds and continually alternate between them.

FAST-SLOW-FAST: Fast out of the glove to 10:00; slow from 10:00 to 2:00; fast from 2:00 to delivery. Specifically, fast motions to 10:00, at which point your body freezes for three-quarers to one full second through the slow stage while your arm keeps moving, until you reach 2:00; then stomp on the gas and throw fast. As you do the slow stage, your stride foot will be hovering above the ground and just a little out in front to balance you.

SLOW-FAST-SLOW: Slow out of the glove to 11:00; fast from 11:00 to 5:30; then put on the brakes from 5:30 to release. In this scenario, we WANT the batter to see you speed up your rotation at 11:00 so she is surprised when you release a slow delivery.

Occasionally, when you can afford to do so, throw a SLOW-SLOW-MEDIUM and WASTE a pitch. Then follow that with a SLOW-FAST and the batter will often stand there, having expected to have more time, and barely twitch as the ball goes by.

After throwing a FAST-SLOW, follow that with one of your fastest pitches and the batter will not know what to expect.

Learning and using this tactic ensures that even the youngest of pitchers can quickly determine how to set up the batters for the next pitching tactic.

You WILL have fun with this but please, do not laugh at the batters. It's, like, really rude!

CHAPTER TWENTY-EIGHT

THE SOFTBALL SUBMARINE WINDUP

Using different pitching style variations, against the same batter is a tactic in a class all to itself. Learning the submarine windup if your normal windup is the double pump, can be a stunningly effective tactic. It can literally freeze a batter in mid-stance.

You set the batter up *with* speed and *for* speed.

You set the batter up *with* ball movement and *for* ball movement.

You set the batter up *with* pitch location and *for* pitch location.

With every pitch you throw, you aim to set the batter up for the *next* pitch.

One way to set the batter up for the next pitch is to implement *different pitching style variations*. Using more than one pitching style variation against a batter can startle the batter to react too late, very badly or even not at all.

Please don't confuse this windup/tactic as being the same as what television baseball announcers refer to as a "submarine style" pitch. Although they have the similar names, they are, in fact, quite different.

When I was very young, pitchers who threw with this submarine windup were referred to as slingshot style pitchers, not submarine style pitchers. There were slingshot pitchers in softball but I have always referred to it as the submarine style in softball.

This submarine windup is easily learned by any pitcher who throws with any pitching style.

Start with the ball in your throwing hand at your side, as if you were taking the call from your catcher. Touch the ball to the inside of your glove then bring the ball back behind you through the bottom half of the windmill circle, to the 12:30 position, just before the ball goes directly over the back of your head. *Do that at the exact same time you take your forward step.*

Reverse direction with the ball and come forward through the bottom part of the windmill circle (the downswing) to delivery, as if it was the last half of your normal windmill circle. Keep your elbow bent at about 45 degrees as you bring the ball behind you.

The secret to this is to start your quick forward step *at the precise moment you are bringing the ball up behind you.* In this way, the timing for both the landing and ball release are the same as your normal pitch with the full windmill windup.

This will be thrown as a step style pitch and not with a big push-off like a leap and drag pitcher uses.

When you bring the ball up behind to the highest point just behind and above the back of your head, the ball should be in front of the hand and facing the batter. Your wrist and the ball will resemble a submarine periscope, except for the bend in the elbow.

TIMING IS CRUCIAL HERE. AT THE INSTANT YOUR LANDING FOOT TOUCHES DOWN, YOU *MUST* HAVE THE BALL CHANGE DIRECTION AS YOU BEGIN THE REAR DOWN-SWING.

If you bring the ball forward to where it is over your head or farther, it will slow you down and you may strain your elbow in the process. So, practice the timing of this slowly at first.

Now, all of this must be done as quickly as possible for the most stunning effect on the batter. This should give you an idea of how fast this must be done:

Without any ball or glove, clap your hands one time as fast as you can, going from the pitcher's position with both hands at your side. Bring your glove hand over to your right side (assuming a right-handed pitcher) and clap your hands near the point where your front right pant pocket would be. Do this a few times as fast as you possibly can. Then do the exact same thing while you take a quick forward step with your stride foot.

Now practice the same thing wearing your glove and with the ball in your throwing hand. Bring the glove over to the throwing hand side and pop the ball in and out just as quickly as possible (just like you were clapping your hands together). Bring the ball back behind you to the 12:30 position and throw a fast pitch from that point. Do all of this *at the same moment* you are taking your forward step. All of the arm motions start at the same moment as the forward step.

This pitch actually starts when you take the call; when you have both hands at your side. The rulebooks allow you to simulate bringing the hands together by touching the glove with the ball as it passes by, with no pause at all.

The rulebooks also state that you must have both feet on the rubber when you separate your hands. This is why you must touch the ball to the inside of the glove instantly as you start the pitch AND as you are starting your forward step. It must be done very, *VERY* quickly.

For a pitcher who normally throws with a double pump windup, this is an awesome tactic because the batters will still be standing there waiting for the rest of your windup.

I have taught this to pitchers in just 15 minutes, between games at their tournaments and, as a result, they have achieved twice the number of strikeouts in their game. Some pitchers may only use

this a handful of times in their game, as a secret weapon, used only when they need it the most to stun a batter.

The most successful pitchers will use this at least once on <u>every</u> batter to ensure they are viewed as completely unpredictable to each and every batter.

Once the other team is uncertain which windup you will use, they will be distracted and remain off balance.

Batters are trained to assume a pitcher uses ONLY ONE pitching style. Why pitch to them EXACTLY as they have been trained to hit? Practice this tactic and use it often. You will quickly learn how effective it is against the batters and how easy it is to set them up. Remember, you can also use the submarine windup in conjunction with variations of the delayed rotation pitch. A fast-slow or slow-fast submarine is an awesome change-up. Throw a fast-slow submarine followed by a submarine fastball and 90% of the batters will stand there slack-jawed and watch as the strike goes by them.

CHAPTER TWENTY-NINE

THE BACK POCKET PUSH WINDUP

This is another stunning tactic. From the instant you bring the ball out of your glove, this windup puts the ball across the plate faster than any other pitching style or windup. But, like everything else I've taught you, it takes practice to do correctly. However, it is very simple to perform.

Bring your hands together, ball in glove. As you separate your hands, bring the ball back only as far as your back pocket; no farther than that.

At the same time, you quickly step off the rubber. You do not *push off* the rubber; you simply take a very fast step.

The instant your stride foot touches down, bring the ball forward quickly and release it as you normally would.

You might even want to come forward with your pivot foot after release. This is the only pitch where walking through the pitch is a good thing. As with every new technique I've taught you, practice this at home before you ever use it in a game. Some very young pitchers may not be able to put enough *push* into it for the ball to reach the plate. Get to where you can do this extremely quickly and accurately before you use it in a game.

This is like taking a very fast step. Do not let the ball go back too far, only as far as your back pocket sits. With practice, you should be able to throw it at about 60% of your fastest speed. However, the ball is released for delivery SO FAST it won't matter that it's only at 60% speed—it will take them totally by surprise.

CHAPTER THIRTY

THE GOODBYE CHANGE-UP

OK. I will admit that this tactic is a distraction tactic and it may bump up against the limit of what's considered acceptable to some umpires.

Whatever slow change you use, whatever grip, whatever pitching style or windup, this technique can be adopted with any of those because it occurs only *after* you release the ball.

Here is how it works. Hold up your throwing hand, fingers spread wide. Now pretend your fingers are the windshield wipers on a car. Wave those fingers back and forth, left to right, two times, as fast as you can. Now hold that hand down by your pivot knee, fingers extended and pointing as close to straight up as you can and, again, wave it back and forth quickly, like a windshield wiper as fast as possible.

That is exactly what I want you to practice doing the instant you release the ball to the batter as a slow change-up: release the ball and drop your hand down by your pivot knee and make that fast windshield wiper motion.

The batters will have locked their eyes on the ball. More than likely, their field of vision will incorporate the same area as your knee. They will be looking so closely that the hand movement will break their concentration on the ball. Congratulations. You've just distracted them. You've taken their eyes off the ball. When that happens it is highly unlikely they will make good contact. Perhaps they may even forget to swing at all.

This will only work if done extraordinarily fast. Any slower and it will have no effect.

Extend those fingers as wide as you can, and execute the wave as quickly after you release the ball as you can. Do not let the wipers wave back and forth more than twice. Two times is sufficient. Any more than twice and you might upset the umpire. You don't want to upset the umpire!

Try this several times in an inning and, when you get good at it, even a few times with your faster pitches as well.

CHAPTER THIRTY-ONE

THE BOOGER FLICK CURVE–THE ULTIMATE UTILITY PITCH

Let me first explain that this pitch got its name from a 12-year-old student of mine several years ago. I had recently shown her what I called my utility pitch, and she was trying to demonstrate to another student the action required of the index finger in this utility pitch. I confess I have yet to come up with a more suitable visual for a young student. The fact that it is so humorous and so visual to kids enables them to *immediately* comprehend what it is I want them to do at the instant of ball release. Therefore, that name has, well, *stuck* after all these years.

This entails gripping the softball with a slight bend in the index finger. You grip the ball so that the tip of the index fingernail lies against the side edge of the seam of one of the legs of the horseshoe. Do not curl the index finger under like you are throwing a knuckleball. Keep just enough pressure on the ball with the index finger to keep that fingernail firmly pressed against the side of the raised seam. You don't want to dig the fingernail into the ball towards the center of the ball. You want to keep as much 'side' pressure against the seam as possible without your finger losing contact and slipping off the seam.

Hold your throwing hand up and make the OK sign, the tips of the index finger and thumb touching to form an O, the other three fingers pointing upward. Place as much pressure against the thumb with your index finger as you can and hold it. Extend your arm and point the other three fingers outward, straight toward your catcher.

Now, this is how this pitch got its name. Pretend that just in front of your index finger, on the side of your thumb, there is a big booger. Flick the booger as hard as you can, as if you were trying to hit your catcher between the eyes from 40 feet away. The index finger "flicks the booger" in this pitch, with the side of the seam being the booger.

You have to admit that it's a pretty effective visual! What the index finger does here at the moment of ball release can produce tremendous ball spin and movement, more than any pitch I have ever seen. By placing the fingertip against the side of the seam on the leg of the horseshoe you produce a seam rotation for maximum disruption of air currents and maximum ball movement.

For a curveball, this pitch is released farther out in front, away from your body, than most other pitches. As the ball passes by the hip, the other three fingers, if extended, would point down toward the ground. As the ball passes the hip, the hand starts rotating counterclockwise (assuming a right-handed pitcher). At the instant the hand rotates, with the index finger pointing flat and directly to the left, the ball is released at the precise moment you "flick the booger." This will take a little practice but not as much as you might think. I have had students pick up on this in as little as six attempts while some practiced for a week to perfect the timing of the release and the flick.

Try it as a slow change-up at first and watch the amount of ball spin you can achieve. It's amazing how much and how early the ball can move. Once you've mastered that, try using the technique at faster speeds. The slower you can throw this, the more ball movement you will get, but excellent ball movement can still be achieved at the faster speeds.

For the slowest speeds, your arm should be extended three-quarters of the way at ball release. Let your hand rotate a little more after you release the ball to avoid stopping the rotation too abruptly.

I stumbled onto this when I was experimenting as a teenager. I discovered that *whatever direction my index finger was pointing when I released the ball was the direction the ball moved*. I then discovered I could use this for a rise ball. I simply rotated my hand slightly inward and released the ball ("flicked the booger," that is) when my index finger pointed straight up. You can throw a curve ball, a rise ball, and everything in between, by simply adjusting where your index finger points when you flick it.

I like this pitch because it produces rise balls and curve balls without stressing any part of a young pitcher's body. There is no extreme rotation, stressing, or snapping of any joint at all, unlike the traditional curve and rise balls.

This is how I've been able to teach students as young as eleven years old to throw these pitches—because they're safe to do and THEY WORK! One grip produces several different movement pitches and none of them stress the young bodies.

CHAPTER THIRTY-TWO

THE ONE-FINGERED KNUCKLEBALL

When I was very young my dad tried to teach me how to throw a knuckleball. His technique was to throw with four fingers bent to where the last knuckles would touching the ball surface, and with his thumb bent, side of the last thumb knuckle applying pressure to the ball for the grip. He would release it WAY out in front with the hand under/behind the ball and basically push the ball with his fingers at the very last moment.

My hand was simply too small to do that. So he tried showing me the two-fingered knuckleball. My hand was almost big enough but not quite—the ball would slip from my grip halfway through the arm circle when I tried to throw it fast. It would dance a little but it was a dead giveaway because I had to slow my arm speed down or risk the ball slipping out of my grip.

I've watched and worked with other pitchers to throw a two-fingered knuckleball and have seen this happen to them too. The ball slips from their grip when they throw with any real speed.

Having had no real success with the two variations my father tried to show me, I started experimenting. At first, I just wanted a grip that produced zero ball spin that I could throw as fast, or nearly as fast, as my fastball.

By my early teens, I discovered that, if I gripped the ball with my fingertips just ABOVE the seam of the round part of the horseshoe, with my thumb lying fairly straight across the ball from my ring finger, that good strong grip allowed me to throw fast with no fear of the ball slipping from my grip.

I brought my middle finger back and placed the tip of it just behind that same seam. From the last knuckle to the tip of my middle finger, it pointed straight toward the center of the ball—NOT curled beneath, like the fingers of a two-fingered knuckleball would be. Only the very tip of the middle finger touched the ball and then only very lightly.

Try this yourself. Note that, when you open your hand and release the ball, the other three fingers should be pointing downward. Open your hand, keeping the middle finger slightly bent and light-

ly touching the ball. The middle finger, being the last finger to touch the ball, will prevent any spin on the ball. This produces a floating knuckleball that's very susceptible to any blowing winds. It tends to break in the same direction as the wind. It can dance a jig even when thrown quite fast.

This was the second-fastest pitch I threw in competition and my catchers hated it. *But the batters hated it even more.* It always moved but was unpredictable, depending on any wind. It might float in and dance a little jig or, it might float in flat and break hard one direction or the other.

The secret to this pitch is to touch the ball with the end of the middle finger without actually applying any pressure. I advise my students to grip it normally, like a softball, with the exception of the middle finger. For the middle finger, they must pretend the ball is an egg they are touching without pressing on it. The key thing, I tell them, is DON'T BREAK THE EGG at *any* point of the pitch.

Keeping good pressure with three fingers and no pressure with the middle finger is often a big challenge for a young pitcher. They must be conscious of the role the fingers are playing in the pitch throughout its entire execution.

To start training a young pitcher to throw this pitch, I will initially use a Wiffle ball. Wiffle balls are like a magnifying glass—they illustrate anything off, and magnify an error 10 times, whether it is a late release point, incorrect finger placement, etc. If not executed perfectly, it will be that much worse when using a Wiffle ball. Practicing with a Wiffle ball is the best way I have found to get a pitcher to think about and realize how important the role her fingers play in the different pitches. You cannot simply muscle the Wiffle ball into the strike zone like you can a regular softball. You have to "finger finesse it" into the strike zone.

Take a felt marker and draw a straight line around the Wiffle ball. Add a horseshoe, and practice throwing the Wiffle ball until you can throw it with zero spin. Then try practicing with a regular softball.

If it is the first time throwing with a Wiffle ball, don't get discouraged and give up. Having good control over what your fingers do does not come instantly to a young pitcher but it can happen very quickly.

This take some practice to master. Once you throw it well with decent control, use the same grip but spread the fingers a little wider and place the tip of the middle finger against the ball the same way but now move it to the right a little to where it is touching the side of the ring finger. This time, because of the slight adjustment of the middle finger, release the ball with the fingers toward the inside of the ball, turning the wrist slightly to the inside. Practice that. This can give your pitch the meanest screwball movement you have ever seen.

There is no follow-through with the throwing arm with this pitch. The hand stops at the release point. If you try and continue the circle and follow through, the other fingers will contact the ball at the very end, giving it unwanted spin.

Good luck and work hard!

CHAPTER THIRTY-THREE

A FEW SNEAKY PLAYS

Here are just a few sneaky plays I have seen used in fast pitch softball.

A runner is on third. The batter lays down a bunt. The catcher goes after the ball. The runner on third has not left the bag. An instant before the catcher touches the ball, the runner on third yells out "Runner!" or "GOING!" as she sprints towards home, takes two steps and stops.

Most of the time, the catcher will, at the very least, hesitate throwing to first, giving the batter/runner an additional second to make it to first base safely.

If the catcher turns toward third and throws, the runner will likely have to dive back but the batter/runner will be safe on first.

At best, the catcher hesitates, makes a hurried throw to first (or third) and the runner on third scores. The batter/runner may or may not make it to second base.

OK. What if we teach the batter to assume that if she swings and misses what would be a third strike, that the catcher has dropped the ball. Even if she swings and misses, she should *always* run to first base. Tell her, "DON'T LOOK! ASSUME IT IS DROPPED AND JUST RUN!"

What if there are no outs and the bases are loaded? If the batter in this scenario still sprints for first, and the catcher reacts by throwing to first, guess what? The third base runner just scored! Now, you tell me: is this sneaky or simply smart base running?

So many times I have seen a dropped third strike where the batter gives up and turns towards the dugout, only to have the catcher scoop up the ball and tag them out by home plate. If the runner had just run, anything might happen. Perhaps the catcher would make a bad throw into right field and now the batter/runner has gotten to second or even third base!

The idea is this: When facing a third strike, if you swing and miss, YOU RUN.

NO EXCEPTIONS, NO HESITATIONS.

THAT IS SIMPLY SMART SOFTBALL.

Is it unethical? I don't think so. Is it sneaky? I suppose it is if you're on the losing side of that play, but you're not, are you? Nope! You're on the smart team!

This potentially sneaky play can only work if your wooden backstop has the wood coming to the sides on different angles:

You, the pitcher, intentionally throw against the left side of the wooden backstop. The second base runner *and the base coaches* see it as a passed ball, the runner sprints for third base with the base coach urging her on. The ball ricochets right back to the catcher who spins sideways, fires the ball to third—the runner is now out at third.

It takes quite a bit of practice to get it down, but it sure is fun to watch! It can also work on a runner trying for second. Try it just once in a game. It rarely works a second time.

Your batter bunts the ball and the runner on second base heads for third. The play is made at third and the runner is safe. The first baseman remains standing close to home plate with the second baseman near the pitcher. The runner on first comes off the bag three steps, feeling very comfortable with the infielders positioned as they are. The third baseman has the ball. She stands up and quickly throws to first base and guess who is there waiting? The right fielder, unnoticed, closed in on first base and catches the ball, tagging out the runner. Nobody noticed her sneak in because all the commotion, all the attention was focused on third base. Third base was where all the action was, where the ball was, and where *everyone* was looking. Sneaky, sneaky!

CHAPTER THIRTY-FOUR

UNKIND THINGS SAID ABOUT A PITCHER

If you practice tactical pitching, the other teams will talk about you. Chances are their comments will NOT be kind. Below is an article I wrote several years ago which I hope will help you deal with that when it happens. Notice, I said *when* it happens, not *if*.

I was probably in my mid teens when I finally figured something out, something I think is pretty important to a young pitcher.

It is a long time proven fact that if you are a pitcher that is worth your salt, people ARE going to be talking about you. If it is someone associated with a team you compete against, chances are some of the things they are going to say will not be very kind or flattering at all.

I had trained myself to be very good at blocking out comments like that so they did not affect me during the game. However, I still heard everything. Many times after the game I would wonder WHY someone had said whatever it was they had said about me personally or about my pitching.

I heard what was said about all the other pitchers too. It took me a few years but what finally educated me to the way it really is, is what I DID NOT HEAR about some of the pitchers.

People would talk a lot about the good pitchers, pitchers they either respected or feared for whatever reason, pitchers they did NOT want to go up against in competition.

People would seldom say much at all, if anything at all, about a pitcher they were not concerned about going up against.

I did not figure it out immediately but I finally realized that all of that talk and all of those unkind remarks about me (and my pitching) were a very great compliment to my ability and my intimidation factor as a pitcher.

As long as they WERE talking about me, they WERE worried about going up against me from the batter's box. If they had ever STOPPED talking like that about me, then I would have started to be worried about my pitching ability.

If you are a young pitcher that is being bothered by unkind comments from the other teams, or cheers that are directed at you, take it as a HUGE compliment. They don't do that to EVERY pitcher, just the good ones that they are very worried about having to face.

I think folks say those unkind words hoping you will hear it or that their comment gets back to you and has an impact on the game you are going throw against their team. They are trying to get into your head. Go ahead and let them but make sure you translate what they say first because anything unkind said about a player can usually be translated to actually mean, "You are good and I don't like that".

Take it as a compliment and be polite, be sure to thank them for saying it with a very pleasant smile on your face.

Trust me, If they DO NOT say something unkind about you or your pitching, you might want to work a little harder on your pitching. If you are really good, they WILL be making unkind comments hoping to get you upset and have an affect on you and your pitching.

As long as they ARE talking (or cheering) about you, you are doing SOMETHING very VERY right! Keep up the good work!

INDEX

Read this NOW!

I've got a FREE Softball Gift for You!

Claim it NOW at:
(Do it NOW before you do anything else or you'll forget!)

www.SendMyFreeSoftballGift.com

Seriously, go claim your FREE gift NOW!

Made in the USA
Charleston, SC
26 October 2011